# HOW TO GET
# A MONKEY
# INTO HARVARD

# HOW TO GET A MONKEY INTO HARVARD

# The Impractical Guide to Fooling the Top Colleges

**Charles Monagan**

**Illustrations by Dave Coverly**

Black Cat
*New York*
a paperback original imprint of Grove/Atlantic, Inc.

*Published simultaneously in Canada*
*Printed in the United States of America*

FIRST EDITION

ISBN-10: 0-8021-7038-2
ISBN-13: 978-0-8021-7038-5

Black Cat
A paperback original imprint of Grove/Atlantic, Inc.
841 Broadway
New York, NY 10003

Distributed by Publishers Group West

www.groveatlantic.com

07 08 09 10 11 12   10 9 8 7 6 5 4 3 2 1

For my own three monkeys: John, Matt, and Claire

# Contents

He takes a folder from the top of the pile, holds it out in front of him and lights it on fire. He watches it burn brightly for a moment before tossing it into a nearby fireplace. "White male soccer captain valedictorian from suburban Connecticut," he says dismissively. "They come in by the dozen – like doughnuts."

# Introduction

The March sunlight floods through the leaded windows in a meeting room of a well-known Ivy League university. It's three days before the final letters go out to high school seniors, and Dirk Ninkman, an assistant dean of admissions who for the moment is alone in the room, takes a slug of Surge and gestures at the stacks of applications on the table before him.

"I think I can speak for my colleagues when I say we honestly don't care at this point," he says wearily. "We have sixteen thousand applications, twenty-six thousand applications—whatever. It's ridiculous. There are five thousand colleges in America and everyone wants to come to this one. And why? Beats me. I *went* here and I still don't understand it. Well, actually, I didn't go here as a *student*. I came for a summer tennis program. But I lived in a dorm and ate in the dining hall, so, uh, it was really pretty similar . . ."

His voice trails off as he takes a folder from the top of the pile, holds it out in front of him and lights it on fire. He watches it burn brightly for a moment before tossing it into the nearby fireplace.

"White male soccer captain valedictorian from suburban Connecticut," he says dismissively. "They come in by the dozen—like doughnuts."

As Ninkman speaks, the rest of the ten-member admissions committee begins to troop in from their lunch break. They have been at it for weeks now, and it's starting to show. One woman, a twelve-year veteran of the process, put on a gorilla head as a joke five days ago; now she wears it all the time. Another has taken to inserting rejection letters into large "acceptance" envelopes along with brochures for community colleges in Idaho. The group trades small talk until the dean of admissions enters the room and takes a seat at the head of the table.

"Let's get back to work," he says, grabbing a folder. And so they do.

First up is a female from a suburban high school in Illinois. White, straight A's, 2200 on her SATs, raises rabbits to sell at Easter, started a volunteer fire department in her town, organized classmates to pipe potable water and electricity into a poverty-stricken rural community. The folder gets passed around.

"Where's the dance piece here?" asks a female voice down the table. "I don't see it."

"Can she do the Watusi?" asks another.

"Or the Swim?"

"How about the Hully Gully or the Locomotion?"

"There's no mention at all of dance that I can recall," says the dean.

"Can she pilot a Zamboni? We need someone who can do that."

"There's nothing here about Zambonis."

"Reject," says the original woman.

There are no defenders.

Next up is a ruddy white male, raised by wolves in northern Canada, unable to speak, but with piercing eyes and a thick, unruly shock of black hair.

"Everyone wants him, of course—all the Ivies," says the dean excitedly. "The question is, 'Can we offer him enough?'"

"What about the language thing?" asks the officer wearing the gorilla head. "Is he willing to learn English?"

"During our interview, he grunted and pounded his hand on my desk twice, which was his way of saying, 'Yes,'" the dean replies, giggling. "And then he peed on the floor."

"Accept," says Ninkman immediately.

"Accept," comes the chorus around the table.

The group next looks at the application of a student from New York City with 1900 SATs, B's and a few C's but straight A's in something his high school calls "Fanglesh." His activities include Pep 'n' Plaid Club and squash (manager). A teacher recommendation says his papers are often fairly entertaining.

The conversation centers for a few moments on what everyone had for lunch, and whether dessert, especially heavy baked goods, at midday is a good idea, before an assistant with a goatee speaks up. "I hate to sound like a boob," he says, "but what's Fanglesh?"

"It caught my eye, too—it must be some sort of combination of French and English," someone else answers vaguely. "Maybe a study of the two languages or cultures—the foods, movies, and so forth. I really don't know."

"If that's the case, wouldn't it be called Franglish?" counters a dean.

"Or Frenglish?" asks another.

There is a long silence around the big table.

"Can we please get back on topic?" asks Ninkman. "I think this is a reasonably strong candidate. He's got some things going for him. Papers that at least one person finds interesting. And you can't ignore those A's, no matter what they're in."

"What does his father do?" someone asks.

"Head of a Fortune 500 corporation," answers the dean.

Admitted.

And so it goes throughout the afternoon. The applicants are admitted, rejected, or placed on the wait list, where they can languish for months, like Japanese soldiers on far-flung islands in the Pacific, before anyone remembers they're there. It's a process that's repeated every spring at selective colleges and universities all across America. As you no doubt realize, the struggle to gain admission to one of the nation's elite schools has never been more difficult. From every high school in every town in every state come dozens of eager, bright, well-qualified graduates, each looking for a place in a prestigious college that their parents are urging them to attend.

Where will your child or children find their places? How will their folders be regarded as they make their way around the conference table? Will they be heckled, laughed at, or set on fire? How will your children face up to the possibility of rejection?

Or, more importantly, how will *you* face up to it? You are the one, after all, who has sacrificed all these years, who has driven selflessly to the soccer fields, the dance studios, and the animal hospital where your daughter nursed sick gerbils back to health so they could once again lead frisky, meaningful lives. You are the one who stood on the sidelines in the freezing cold and applauded *all* the children on *both* teams, no matter how poorly they played. It was you who cut the oranges into sections, who struggled to insert the straws into the juice boxes, and who made sure everyone took home a stupid little trophy. You are the one who relearned algebra so you could literally do the homework when your child was too busy, who memorized over two thousand vocabulary words so you could conduct pop quizzes in the car, and who expertly bad-mouthed other children as Awards Day approached.

And now it is time for your ultimate test: to get your child into a very good, or at least very expensive, college. To do so, you must first understand that the admissions-committee drama at the beginning of this chapter really happened. Last spring, for $350 and a promise not to mention the huge boil on the back of one dean's neck, I was granted unparalleled access to the admissions process at an Ivy League school. It was my feeling that only by getting behind the heavily guarded gates of academia could I truly begin to see what an admissions committee considers, and frankly how irresponsible and arbitrary it can be, as it selects an incoming freshman class. As I sat in, I witnessed every eye-opening part of the process, including a fire drill and a series of bomb threats that turned out to be part of one applicant's effort to attract attention to his cause (he was admitted).

I have put in the time backstage. Beyond my brief stay at that one particular college, I have also traveled extensively across the country, probably to the very campuses you and your child are considering, and I've spoken to the people in charge. Now I want to pass what I've learned on to you so that you can take full ownership of your own admission process. In this guide, I'll cover all the essentials you'll need to construct a plausible application for your high school graduate, and I'll also touch on some of my more remarkable findings, such as:

—The "secret handshake" that assures admission to any top college
—The former U.S. president who will write you a recommendation for $100
—The key that once unlocked all the SAT analogies
—The perfect opening line for your interview (and how much to tip at the end)

So let's get started. As we speak, résumés are being built and your child is falling behind. In Utah, there's a high school senior who's putting together the nation's first all-wheelchair marching band; in Ohio, an all-state wrestler is voluntarily (well, his parents are making him do it) living for a year in a mental hospital to buttress his extracurricular piece; in Maryland, a brilliantly contrarian seventeen-year-old has made big-game hunting and taxidermy his "passion," and is loading the stuffed and mounted heads of antelopes, big cats, rhinos, etc. into a U-Haul for his upcoming tour of college campuses. Are you up to the challenge? You will be if you read and take to heart all that follows. Good luck.

**Space Shuttle Parents.** They fly together with their child, at least for a while. *"We got 1200 on the SATs,"* you'll hear them say. *"We just got into Bowdoin."*

# 1

# Getting Started

## Off on the Long Road Together

"Mom, Dad! I'm being recruited!"

The words echo through the house. It's your child, a high school junior. He rushes in from his room, holding high a sheet of paper he's just grabbed from his printer. He smiles broadly as he hands it over. It's a copy of an e-mail.

"Obtiain a prosperous future," the e-mail says. "Money earning power. Get a diploma based on your experience call now to recieve diploma in 2 wks (call 24hrs, 7 day's a week) deciduous chauffeur circulant Calcutta casino Britain bequeath circumlocution [signed] sceptic."

And so the marvelous process of college admission has begun. Your child, the one you began prepping for a top college when he was still in his crib, may not be bright enough to know the difference between Internet spam and a genuine recruiting pitch, but that's not the point. The point is that he's showing the first spark of interest. *At last.* Now it's time for you—you who have been rowing relentlessly upstream, waiting for just such a moment—to really get to work.

But first a little history.

Many years ago, getting into a good college was a simple matter (as long as you were a Caucasian male, preferably Protestant). Someone with a white mustache spoke to someone else wearing a pocket watch and it was done. Once safely ensconced on campus, students in those days were perfectly happy getting C's and D's, hitting each other with paddles, smoking pipes, and learning a few useful aphorisms in Latin before going off to run banks and eat oysters for lunch.

Even when you, the parent of today's applicant, were applying to schools, the process, in fact the whole college scene, was vastly simpler and more relaxed than it is now. Pot was so cheap that everyone on campus, including the entire admissions office, was stoned all the time, and—feeling very mellow and gentle— was susceptible to even the slightest nudge of pressure from an anxious parent. Slackers could still get in if their connections were solid or if they had cool bushy hair or wore a hip T-shirt to their interview. The SATs were low-key affairs. AP courses were unheard of. Community service was still something criminals did in order to reduce their jail time, not something high school students grudgingly did, or pretended to do, to polish their résumés.

But now, as you no doubt have long been aware, admission to a top college is getting more difficult every year. It has been estimated that the number of high school graduates in the United States will peak during the years 2007–2011, and God only knows what's going on in places like South Korea, India, and other countries that send supercharged swarms of their top students to American colleges. According to school and government officials, this historic rise in potential applicants is due to a number of factors:

—Unprotected sex
—Suggestive programming on TV shows and in video games

—Smoking
—The left-leaning media

Whatever the reasons, with ever-larger numbers of overquali-
fied students applying for a fixed number of openings, colleges
are forced to become increasingly cagey and sly about how they
admit applicants. Even someone with my impeccable connections
will never know what happened at Georgetown, for instance,
when, in 2006, it got over two thousand applicants who not only
had perfect SAT scores and were ranked number one in their high
school class, but who had recently gone to communion and were
still in a state of grace when they came to tour the campus. And
what did Stanford do with the nearly twelve hundred applicants
for the Class of 2010 who were not only highly attractive but
whose parents had made millions in the high-tech industries of
nearby Silicon Valley?

"The application pool is so strong, we just cast our nets blindly,"
admits one director of admissions. "But the well-played gimmick,
the clever ploy, the expensive gift—whatever you want to call it—
can really set someone apart."

"I see these applications from superbly talented students," says
another top dean, "and I think the same thing as when I see all
the teenage girls who pose nude on the Internet: Who are these
fantastic young people? How come I never knew anyone like that
when I was growing up?"

## Why a Top College?

It is the assumption of *How to Get a Monkey into Harvard* that
you, the parent, are engaged in the process of trying to get your
in-many-respects-unexceptional child into a very good school, or
at least one that most people think is very good. As you proceed
down this road, you may find obstacles rising in your way (as when
your "little one" sneaks off to Argentina to meet an Internet se-
ducer), but I am here to emphasize that you must never lose sight

of your goal. Your efforts are well worth it. The benefits of going
to a top college are many, and they are getting more pronounced
every day. Here are just a few of the most obvious advantages:

**It's almost impossible to get kicked out of a top college.**
It may be hard to get in, but almost no one ever gets asked to
leave. This was true in 1890 and in 1950, and it remains true now.
And even if a student totally screws up and has to drop out, he or
she can often be readmitted at a later date. Do not underesti-
mate this benefit.

**Cocktail party credibility.** Graduates of top colleges don't
wear pins telling others where they went to school (well, actually, some do), but they can be very good at quickly heading a
first-time conversation in that direction. "Oh, you're from Philadelphia?" you'll hear them say. "Well, I guess it's a small world,
because I spent four years in New Haven at Yale." Once this little
college game has been played and won, the buzz from the cock-
tails becomes a secondary thrill.

**If they want to, Harvard graduates can go to work writ-
ing for *The Simpsons* or David Letterman upon leaving
school.** This lends a great feeling of security to undergrads when
they think about the future, sort of like having a good back-up
college you know you can get into. What is less well known is that
other top schools have similar pipelines into other TV shows.
Columbia grads write gags for Emeril, Larry King gets his quips
from recent Rice alums, and a notorious "boys only" cabal from
Penn keeps The Weather Channel's on-air personnel well stocked
with witticisms and meteorological metaphors.

**More money.** Enter the world of business armed with a diploma from a top college and watch employers fall over each other
with offers of money, money, and still more money. While grads
from inferior schools struggle with rent and car payments, Ivy
grads and others like them are summering in the Hamptons and
ordering up chilled bottles of Cristal at sleek metropolitan watering holes. Is this because they're smarter or more capable than
their confreres? C'mon, have you *seen* these people? It's all about
the colleges they went to—colleges your child can go to as well.

## Identifying a Top College

Once you've decided a top school is the right choice for your child, the next step is figuring out which ones are suitably "top." You can go by SAT scores, of course, or magazine ratings or other traditional indicators, but I have found that the following list works just as well:

| Top | Not |
|---|---|
| Nice old chapel | Huge new chapel |
| Classy Latin Motto | Cheesy Latin Motto |
| Veritas Harvard | Adrianum Collegium Adrianiae—Adrian College |
| Gothic arches | Golden arches |
| Ivy | Cactus |
| Merit scholars | Merit smokers |
| Fireplaces in dorm rooms | Fires in dorm rooms |
| Ski team | Water ski team |
| Carillon plays Bach | Carillon plays Lionel Richie |

## Defining the Parent's Role

Perhaps you saw the story that appeared recently in newspapers across the country:

### Parent Admitted To Tufts

The mother of a suburban Chicago high school senior was admitted to Tufts University after school officials determined it was she, and not her son, who really wanted to go there.

Anna Leary Stimson, 49, has not yet decided what she'll do about this unexpected turn of events, although she did admit to being "a little bit embarrassed" by the fuss she's kicked up.

"I got a little too caught up in the process," she said. "I just got carried away. I mean, as I look back on it now, I dominated the interview during our campus visit, and in the essay I guess I wrote about things he never could have experienced or remembered, like getting a swine flu shot."

The article went on predictably from there to attack the growing cadre of parents who believe some aggression is called for these days in dealing with the college-admission process.

Still, we can learn from Ms. Stimson's example. You *can* go too far. Or more to the point, you can get *caught* going too far. A good, basic rule of thumb is that you don't want your ambition for your child, however justified it may be, to turn into a news story. We all know about the parents who force their seven-year-olds to fly solo across the Atlantic, or irate dads who go after Little League umpires with aluminum baseball bats. That kind of behavior is not what this book is about. We want to maintain a thin veil of civility at all times—or at least until a clear knockout blow can be delivered.

But first of all, you must decide what sort of parent you are, and into which general group you fall. I realize that none of us likes to be categorized, but it really can be helpful in this case. Once you recognize yourself and your grouping, it's easier to find others of the same feather as you make the rounds in this college process. Who better to listen to your "war" stories or commiserate with your struggles than one of your fellow travelers? I have come up with a host of terms to cover the many styles of parenting I have encountered during my years in this field. Here are a few of the more common ones:

**Helicopter Parents.** These are the ones we all know about. They hover, sometimes quite noisily, over their children and all their children's activities. They are driven by the intense desire not only that their children do well, but that others do poorly, and that proper and full credit is given at the end of the day. Examples of notable Helicopter Parents abound throughout history. One splendid "chopper" was Mary Pinkney Hardy MacArthur, the mother of World War II hero General Douglas MacArthur. As her son (and she) applied for admission to West Point in the late 1890s, Mrs. MacArthur gathered recommendations from thirteen governors, senators, congressmen, and bishops (although

President Grover Cleveland declined). To further the cause, she moved with young Douglas away from her husband to a congressional district in Wisconsin, where the local congressman was a friend of the family and thus apt to be helpful. When Douglas was finally admitted to West Point, she went with him, living for four years in a nearby hotel from which she could keep an eye on his dorm room window. Other famous Helicopters in American history include Helen Stevenson, who went to live right down the street from her little Adlai when he went to Princeton, and Sarah Delano Roosevelt, who went to live in Cambridge when Franklin went off to Harvard.

**Hummingbird Parents.** They hover, but not as noisily as the Helicopters. They are not as apt to ask loud, self-centered questions during college information sessions, preferring to quietly approach the speaker later, over cookies and punch.

**Dragonfly Parents.** They hover in tandem, but dart off into the shadows to have sex every once in a while.

**Pile Driver Parents.** These half-crazy moms and dads are more often found in the sports world than in the college-admissions game. The father of tennis star Mary Pierce was an exemplary Pile Driver before he was banned from watching her compete. He once shouted from the stands during a match: "Go on, Mary, kill the bitch!" As the admissions race continues to heat up, Pile Drivers may become more commonplace.

**Space Shuttle Parents.** They fly together with their child, at least for a while. "*We* got 2100 on the SATs," you'll hear them say. "*We* just got into Bowdoin."

**Penguin Parents.** Their specialty is regurgitating information for their child. They open all college correspondence, no matter to whom it's addressed, so they can properly interpret what's inside and ensure that a response is sent off when it's required. Likewise, Penguins distill and retain hours of Internet research for later consumption and even rephrase questions college officials may ask their children during campus visits.

**Albatross Parents.** Hopelessly out of it. They're usually significantly older than the other parents and, if truth be told, lost interest in their child—and parenting in general—back when their kids were in the fifth grade. Now they are trying to make up for lost time with a gaudy show of interest during the college-admission process. Even so, Dad tends to fall asleep during information sessions and Mom can't get past coed dorms.

**Zeppelin Parents.** Insist on listening to 1960s rock music while driving to and from campus visits.

No matter what sort of parent you are (and I hope you found a group to relate to), remember: we're all in this process together. Before I move on, I'd like to leave you with one more set of useful general guidelines:

## Keys for Parents in the College Admission Process

**Start discussing college in serious terms as soon as your child is able to speak and understand.** And before that, don't forget that even a tiny baby can respond to visual signals. Get an Ivy League mobile—featuring a bobbing symbol of each of the eight schools—to hang over her crib, or an oversized stuffed mascot that can become her first "friend." Along these same lines, when naming your child, be sure to give consideration to the middle name. There's no law against using Rockefeller or Mellon or even Yale or Vanderbilt—although naming a boy Elihu or Cornelius is probably going too far *(or is it?)*.

**Never let up.** Emphasize to your child the importance of beating out friends and winning the "game" of getting into one of the most selective schools. In so doing, don't be afraid, as a parent, to be a little selfish: view the college selection and application process as a matter of helping *you* reach an outcome *you* will value and that *you* can brag about to *your* friends.

**Allow the college-admissions process to take over your family's life.** Welcome it. Nurture it. Bring SAT vocabulary quizzes to the dinner table. Use peas and rosary beads to demonstrate mathematical theorems. Pressure all the family members, including cousins and in-laws, to pitch in to make the candidate's extracurricular project—knitting Free Tibet–themed booties for inner-city preemies—a success.

**Take control of the college-application process, but be sure not to let any "outsiders" know.** Schedule everything, do homework, type applications, write essays, disguise your voice to make admissions phone calls. The truth is, you can't trust anyone, and certainly not your child, to do the job as well as you can do it.

**Remain adamant about getting your child into an "out-of-reach" school.** All you need to do is look around a little bit (as I'm sure you've been doing) to find plenty of unworthy students who've gotten into outstanding schools. How does this happen? Who, or what, do you have to know? What's the secret password? Actually, there are lots of them. At one school, it might be the adept use of a gerund, at another a single yellow rose, at a third, if you've got the nerve, simply standing in the admissions office and intoning, "Open sesame!" We'll be discussing some of these strategies later in the book.

**Marry your child's college counselor.** It doesn't have to be a long-term, lovey-dovey thing, just a good workable relationship with lots of gifts and sex.

**Whatever the outcome, spin the results.** You've heard that Stanford is the Harvard of the West and Duke is the Yale of the South, but did you know that the University of Georgia is the Cornell of the Southeast, Emory is the Middlebury of Atlanta, Pepperdine is the Tulane of the Pacific, Miami of Ohio is the Loyola of Chicago of Ohio, and the University of New Mexico is the University of Arizona of New Mexico? There's a whole world of spin out there, you just have to learn the language.

So, are you ready to move on? I certainly hope so, because your child isn't going anywhere without your help. Let's begin by attacking that pesky high school curriculum.

"To tell you the truth," confided one dean, "if a kid has the nerve to wear a sombrero into his interview, in my mind that outweighs any holes he might have in his course load."

# 2

# Academics and Résumé Building

## Making the Grades

"One of the big mistakes that ambitious high school students make is studying hard. I'm not saying they shouldn't study. They just don't have to study *hard*."

These words were spoken to me by a meerschaum-puffing admissions officer at a fashionable small college in Pennsylvania —but they were more or less repeated everywhere I went on my *Monkey* tour of American campuses. The fact is, these days admissions committees at top colleges are so overwhelmed by applications that while they might get a chance to glance at your child's grades, they really don't have the time to figure out how difficult the courses were, how rigorous the school is, or how dedicated the faculty is. In other words, you can forget the stress of AP courses and tests, forget difficult honors seminars, forget Latin and those math courses that use little symbols and squiggles instead of numbers. Begin advising your child now—right now— to find the easiest teachers and take the easiest courses he or she can find.

"Difficult high school courses have pretty much lost their significance," confided another dean. "To tell you the truth, if a kid has the nerve to wear a sombrero into his interview, in my mind that outweighs any holes he might have in his course load."

Once you realize that an A in Introductory Keyboarding carries roughly the same weight as an A in AP World History, it becomes much easier for you and your child to draw up the ideal high school curriculum. Here's a course-load lead you might want to follow:

| | |
|---|---|
| **9th Grade** | Gym |
| | Introductory Keyboarding |
| | Open Period |
| | Theater (Props) |
| | General Awareness |
| **10th Grade** | Gym II |
| | Intermediate Keyboarding |
| | Idiomatic English |
| | Driver's Ed |
| | Health: Sexually-Transmitted Diseases |
| **11th Grade** | Gym III |
| | Advanced Keyboarding |
| | Pet Grooming |
| | Art for Athletes |
| | Weather |
| **12th Grade** | AP Gym |
| | Honors Keyboarding |
| | General Masonry |
| | CPR/Heimlich |
| | Driver's Ed II (trucks and heavy machinery) |

If your child follows this outline, he should easily achieve "top decile status" (perfect for increasingly bottom-line oriented admission committees) while still having plenty of time to fill in the rest of his résumé, work full time, and possibly even run for elective office. Indeed, while students applying to the Ivies, the Little Ivies, the Hidden Ivies, the Recumbent Ivies, the Alabama Ivies, and the Discount Ivies are up late at night with loads of homework, lab reports, and oral presentations to worry about, your child can be peacefully drifting off to sleep, listening yet again to the difference between "ascetic" and "aesthetic" on your homemade vocabulary tapes.

## Advanced Placement Courses

One of the great challenges and pleasures for high school students used to be trying to get their teachers to wander off on entertaining tangents that had nothing to do with course work. If I might get personal for a moment, long ago I had a history teacher who was an enormous Detroit Tigers fan and it was possible, especially in spring, to get him talking Tigers baseball for two or three days at a time. "How could pitcher Mickey Lolich be so fat and still so good?" we'd ask him. "Is Gates Brown really the best pinch hitter in all of baseball?" Sometimes a Tigers question would even show up for extra credit on a test. It was fun for us, fun for him—a win, win situation—and when the Tigers finally won, it was win, win, win.

The AP courses have ruined all that. High school teachers these days are increasingly forced to "teach to the test" and thus can't spare even a few moments for a goofy diversion. As the testing date approaches each spring, AP classrooms all across America become sweaty, highly charged pressure-cookers where jabbering, wild-eyed teachers spew out reams of data and hand out colossal reading assignments while students grunt and squeal and pull out hanks of their own hair. What students will ever look back fondly on those days? Not many (especially if their hair never grows back).

For the reasons cited in the previous section, you can feel confident that your child needn't bother with AP courses. But if you're still not convinced, please answer something for me: what good are the AP courses? Who cares if your child gets to skip an introductory college course? Remember: *getting in* to the college is the thing here. What happens after that really doesn't matter.

## The High School Helper Homework Help

With all the extracurricular activities your child is engaged in, not to mention all the instant messaging and video gaming and hanging out, how can he or she be expected to have time for homework? That being said, won't it be fun to learn all about the Stamp Act and the Battle of Oyster Bay again?

As you labor over your child's textbooks, here are a few things to keep in mind:

—What you are doing is not illegal. There's no law that says you can't do your child's homework. No one's going to break down your front door and take you away in handcuffs and leg shackles or parade you in front of television cameras or discuss your situation on a cable "news" program (unless you've been doing the homework of a daughter who's blonde and attractive).

—Writing like a smart child is different from writing like a dumb adult.

—It's actually amusing to see how long you can keep Charles's law, Planck's constant, and Bernoulli's principle straight in your head—if you can understand them at all. (And where, you may ask, does Boyle's law fit in? And did these distinguished scientists all know each other? Did they socialize? Did their wives get along?)

—Be sure to eat well and get plenty of sleep. High schools are giving out more homework than ever and you don't want fatigue to become a factor.

## The Community College Option

Admissions officers are impressed any time an applicant shows "reach" that goes beyond the normal high school curriculum.

We all know of super-motivated high school students who either take special, "college level" courses or actually enroll at a nearby reputable college in order to pursue an especially demanding course load in, say, Chinese or Physics. With this in mind, I suggest that you and your child explore the blessedly easy courses offered by your local community college. If you can find a few to take, complete, and add to your child's academic résumé, you will have gained an enormous advantage over the competition while exerting almost no effort at all. I recently picked up a course guide at the community college near where I live and found a few courses that look very doable, to say the least:

**Language Arts**   *Conversational English.* "What time is it?" "Where is the library?" "Sir, your daughter is very beautiful!" These phrases and many more are explored and repeated over and over until you learn them.

**Mathematics**   *Introduction to Introductory Mathematics.* Is it time to make a fresh start with the basics? Here, you'll get ready to revisit old friends addition, subtraction, multiplication, and division—and put them into real-world situations as you divide tips and ante up for poker hands.

**The Arts**   *Listening to Music.* Did I hear a banjo in that Coldplay song? Do hand claps and soulful whistling really assure success on the pop charts? You and a former FM-radio deejay (TBA) draw the lines that connect Bach and rock and Bacharach.

**Life Skills**   *Not Dressing With Your Underpants Showing.* This course specializes in practical information and advice to help the student make his or her way in the world of adults.

## Home Schooling

The search by leading schools for strange kids with significant problems (and equally troubled parents) finds a natural match with applicants who have been schooled at home. This is where we find five-year-old kids spouting long Bible passages in German to parents wearing aviator-style glasses (him) and Amish blouses buttoned up to the neck (her). It's where fourteen-year-old college applicants can cover the philosophical waterfront from Plato to Satchel Paige but can't cross a busy street unless they're in a harness.

In other words, it's a world of dysfunction that "gives us a reason for doing what we do," according to one top-college admissions officer. Here's what several of her colleagues had to say about some of their home-schooled applicants:

"I love them all, but imitating bird songs, however beautifully, just can't take the place of geometry and algebra."

"Sometimes the girls remind me of Carrie and their mothers remind me of Carrie's mother. I'm afraid if I don't recommend acceptance, they're going to return to campus and choke me with a fire hose."

"They're so used to fighting city hall and the local school board that parrying and thrusting with a college admissions office is nothing to them. They pretty much bend us to their will."

"The thing that bothers me most about these kids is that they don't know what a sloppy joe is. They've never eaten one—never even been inside a high school cafeteria. How can you say you're ready for college, or *life* for that matter, when you've never heard of a sloppy joe?"

## Building the Résumé

There's no getting around it: top colleges say they want more than just straight A's. In order to build an impressive college-admission résumé that an admissions officer might actually look at, a seventeen-year-old has to get involved in a great many questionable activities outside of the classroom—or inflate routine activities, like taking out the garbage or feeding the goldfish, to the point that they seem like special talents. Here are several of the major résumé areas and what your child might do to make them shine.

## Sports

A graduating high school senior doesn't have to be a future professional athlete or an Olympian to get admitted to the college of his or her choice, but it really, really, *really* helps. Remember, though, when it comes to athletics and future stardom, we're not talking about your child. We're talking about a terrific athlete in a good high school program, not a skinny shortstop who bats .240 or a pretty good JV soccer goalie—no matter how great she was in third grade. It's time to face the fact that if your child is a top athlete, you know it and all the colleges know it. If not, you'll have to come up with a different sort of "athletic" angle for the résumé. Here are a few that I know have worked:

*Managing.* Can your child stick a water bottle into a sweaty athlete's mouth, dry off a wet football, or trail a college coach up and down the sideline making sure the wires from his headset don't get tangled? You may have a future sports manager in your house! Get to work now on towel management, sprinting onto the field during time-outs while carrying a big tray of Gatorade, and handing out jocks to jocks without blushing.

*Mascotry.* Every college needs a mascot that runs out on the court, leads the cheers, taunts the opposing mascot, ogles coeds, or generally screws around during sporting events. Very few admissions committees hear from applicants who aspire, while still in high school, to be that college's mascot. Would it be crazy for your child to keep a "mascot scrapbook" to show the admissions officer when he comes for his campus interview? Maybe. But it might just be crazy enough to be effective.

*Really Stupid Sports.* At one point not so long ago, it was still possible to get into a top college by merely playing one of the former "fringe" sports, such as lacrosse, rowing, or girls ice hockey. By now, however, those sports have been thoroughly discovered by ambitious college-bound students and their parents, so it's necessary to look even further afield for athletic opportunities. Luckily, the truly great colleges and their forward-looking students like to be among the first to welcome amusing new sports to their campuses. For instance, who ever thought Ultimate (also known as Ultimate Frisbee) would grow into a full-fledged intercollegiate sport from something drug-addled slackers did on nice spring days when they should have been in class? Assuming this deterioration of what qualifies as a sport continues in the years ahead, let's think of an activity that's yet to be exploited but in which your unathletic child still might claim expertise. Could miniature golf be the next big thing? Or video poker? How about Beer Pong or Spider Solitaire? It's time for your applicant to get creative and move out ahead of the sports curve just a bit.

## Student Government

As with valedictorians and salutatorians, school and class presidents are a dime a dozen in the college-admissions game. So are vice presidents, treasurers, secretaries, sergeants at arms, majority whips, judicial committee members, hall monitors, precinct captains, ward heelers, and any other position a high school might dream up to make more of its students feel special.

Consequently, running for and serving in student government is really a big waste of time. However, if your child were to stage a coup, bloodless or otherwise, overthrow the current smiley-face student-government regime, and install a no-nonsense junta at his or her high school and get *USA Today* to cover it . . . well then, that's something an admissions group would have to pay attention to.

## Academic Honors

Have you *seen* the honor rolls published in your local news paper lately? (Of course you have.) Does anyone not get honors? There are Faculty Honors, Top Honors, Second Honors, Third Honors, Honorable Mention, and just plain Mention. Who are all these hundreds of unworthy children? How is a college-admissions committee supposed to pick out your child from the mob of pretenders and view her as separate and special?

The thing to do is to look beyond those listings in the newspaper and try to break through with a real-world achievement.

Is your child a good writer? Have her write a book and then have a family friend nominate it for a National Book Award.

Is she good at physics? Have her do a report on strategies for playing the loop-de-loop at the local miniature golf course and then have a family friend nominate her for a Nobel Prize in Physics.

Can she swim the length of a pool (or even just the width)? Have a family friend nominate her for the National Swimming & Diving Hall of Fame.

The point is, anyone can be nominated for a high honor. Your child's nomination may be completely without merit, but "Nominated for a Pulitzer Prize" or "Nominated for a MacArthur 'genius grant'" still looks very good on a college-admissions résumé.

## Community Service

The world of college admissions might thrive on inflated claims and dubious achievements, but nothing in the application process comes close to the truly fraudulent realm of community service. This is a place where watering geraniums in a downtown sidewalk planter, serving a sandwich or two in a homeless shelter, or washing cars in support of the local pet shelter is pushed forward as a sign of selflessness and nobility—something that will separate one special child from the common herd.

Well, of course every high school student claims some form of community service these days in order to make a better résumé for college. And as long as *they're* lying (which they are), you may

as well advise your child to stretch the truth her- or himself.
Here's how it might come up in an interview.

Admissions officer: "I see you've devoted a good portion of
your time to community service. Can you tell me about that?"

Student: "Well, with 9-11, Katrina, whatever . . . I built houses
for, um, Habitat of Humidity."

Admissions officer: "Do you mean 'for *Humanity*'?"

Student: "Well, really, yeah, thanks . . . I guess it was for
humanity."

Admissions officer: "And it says here you built them by
yourself."

Student: "Well, not the first one. But after that, I was pretty
much on my own. I did need some help installing the dishwash-
ers and the skylights. And paving the driveways. I'm not too cool
with that blacktop stuff."

Admissions officer: "That must have taken an enormous
amount of your time."

Student: "Yeah, but I was like, 'Do I want my grades to suffer
or do I want *people* to suffer.' Dude, I had no choice. I had to let
the grades go for a bit."

(Admissions officer quietly checks off the Accepted box on his
notepad.)


## Jobs

The problem here is that with so many high school students traveling around the world, or taking expensive enrichment courses,
or pushing paper at puffed-up internships, or helping out at
social-service agencies, or just hanging around the house
while their parents do their homework, they don't have time
for real jobs anymore. The grocery baggers, newspaper car-
riers, and soda jerks of yesteryear have been replaced by kids
who go to golf camp or ride shotgun in a needle-exchange
van.

Admittedly, admissions officers will barely look at what jobs an applicant has had, but it's always a good idea to have something written under the Employment heading. If your child is coming up short in this area, I'd suggest any of these useful filler positions:

*Private Vehicle Operator.* Facilitated four-wheel transport of school-aged children to various daytime and evening locations. Managed purchase, pick-up, and delivery of critical quotidian supplies from commercial and retail locations to domestic hub. Knowledge of local transportation grid, fuel-supply systems, cabin heating, and cooling controls, etc.

*Media Consultant.* Technical facilitator for the safe and successful operation of a variety of domestic communication, informational, and entertainment devices. Knowledge of both terrestrial and satellite-based systems, anode/cathode packages, and electrical socketry.

## Hobbies and Special Talents

Here it's important to distinguish true talent from mere peculiarity, and an impressive hobby from something that's just scary. For example, your son or daughter may be able to drive a car backward just by using the rearview mirror, or toss peanuts high into the air and catch them in his or her mouth, or always win at Rock, Paper, Scissors, but are these really talents that a college-admissions committee would be interested in? If, on the other hand, your young applicant can toss peanuts high into the air and catch them in his or her *nose*, that's obviously worth putting high on the résumé.

Likewise with hobbies. Your child's traditional collection of stamps, rocks, or coins won't mean much, but a good assortment of swizzle sticks or tilted shot glasses from beachside bars in the Caribbean might impress some of the younger admissions officers. Better yet, does your child like to repair Volvos? Whether he does or not, put it on the résumé. That's a hobby that does very well with admissions committees.

## Hidden Paths to Admission

There are many campus niches—each necessary to a happy, well-ordered college community—that admissions committees secretly seek to fill, but that are almost never known to or thought of by even the most ambitious applicants. From the list of résumé-builders below, perhaps your child can find something valuable to bring to the incoming freshman class, and thus virtually guarantee admission.

**—Always being the first to finish an important exam.** Must be willing to finish so ridiculously early that the other students taking the exam laugh and applaud. This selfless act, especially if it's repeated in exam after exam, inserts an important moment of levity to an otherwise pressure-filled exercise and makes for a happier student population.

**—Know all the words to all the school songs.** There are moments in the life of a college (such as when an elderly and very loyal and wealthy alum is present) when a rousing rendition of the alma mater or a football fight song seems to be in order. If your child can demonstrate an ability and willingness to practice this disappearing art, admission is yours.

**—Design and wear dresses made from crime-scene tape or Ace bandages.** Admissions committees love eccentrics, feeling they add a sense of drama and cutting-edge absurdity to a campus otherwise populated by drones and stupid jocks.

**—Dream up clever but harmless pranks to pull on rival schools.** This talent is already considered a legitimate résumé item at MIT, but other schools have yet to catch up. Can you somehow get the Yale Bulldog to show up in the background of one of al-Qaida's terrorist-training tapes? If so, you're in at Harvard. Can you make the Army Mule blow bubbles out of its ass on national TV during the Macy's Thanksgiving Day parade? The U.S. Naval Academy wants you!

**—Promise to go to church.** The loneliest place on many top-but-essentially-godless college campuses these days is the chapel. Make a deal with the admissions committee: if they let you in, you'll pray for them.

### Enrichment Programs

How much money do you have to spend? That's the basic question posed by summer enrichment programs aimed at college-bound students. Do you have enough to send your child to a leafy boarding school campus, where she can play tennis, meet boys, dabble in Human Geography, and exclude girls who have accents? Or maybe you have enough cash lying around to back an overseas program to a Spanish-speaking Caribbean island that features rum drinks, satellite TV, and shuttles to shopping bazaars? Needless to say, busy college admissions committees think very little of such junkets. Much wiser to save your money to help your child socialize at college by funding his or her Freshman Week card games.

However, special attention should be paid when the president of the United States invites your child to come to Washington, D.C., apparently to help him lead the country and the world out of its current doldrums. The invitation comes in an impressively large and thick envelope with your child's name and address written in what at first glance appears to be genuine calligraphy. Inside, on rich stationery replete with gold seals and etchings of the White House, the U.S. Treasury, and Mount Vernon, your "young global leader" is invited to attend conferences, tour embassies, see "awe-inspiring" monuments, visit Budapest, meet high-ranking government officials, retrace the footsteps of former rulers, and get jiggy with other horny young teen-aged leaders from all over the world. Could this possibly be legit? Could your child, the one who can't clean her hair out of the bathtub drain, actually be a "young global leader"? Just take a look at the long list of U.S. senators and representatives who serve as the program's Board of Advisors—and, *holy cow*, look at how the stationery is *embossed!*

As you turn through the pages, however, imagining your child in such an exalted setting, keep a couple of things in mind: 1) Her chances with a particular college rise much, much more rapidly if she attends its own summer enrichment program, and 2) as you may have noticed in the invitation's small print, "Enrollment in the program is on a space available basis and enrollments are processed in the order they are received. Payment is due with the enrollment form."

They don't call them enrichment programs for nothing.

**Make your child stand by your side, and every time he defines a word properly you feed him a fish from a small pail at your feet.**

# 3
# Standardized Testing

## The New SATs

The more the SATs have been criticized for being biased, irrelevant, and ridiculous, the more importance college admissions departments have placed upon them. This perverse situation was brought home most vividly by an admissions dean at a highly regarded Midwestern liberal-arts college who recently confided to me, "If we got rid of standardized testing, it would mean we'd actually have to examine the applications; if we had to do that, everyone in the admissions department would quit, no matter how many of those milk-carton thingies of Goldfish we brought into the conference room. The truth is, the *only* thing we look at here are SAT scores—other than celebrity recommendations, of course."

Not ones to leave a good enough thing alone, the mahatmas at SAT headquarters in Princeton have recently instituted major changes in the tests. Just in time for the 2004–05 season, they removed the beloved analogies and an obscure area of math that no one cared about or understood, and introduced a writing

31

sample and a new area of math that no one feels comfortable talking about. What's more, gone is the old scoring system, the 1000-to-1600 range that became the touchstone for millions of conversations over the past fifty years in which one party was trying to get the measure of the other. Now the range is more like 1500 to 2400, and it will take parents a while to reach a comfort zone before bragging about or sidestepping the new numbers. In any case, with so much attention focused on the revamped SAT test, it's time for a basic refresher.

## What Are the Tests?

The SAT, also called the SAT I, is a long test with many, many numbingly difficult math questions, lots of hair-splitting sentence completions and reading-comprehension passages about farming. The test is used to find out how smart students are and to get them into or rejected by top colleges.

The SAT II tests used to be called Achievement Tests. They are concerned with specific subjects, but they aren't much different from the SATs in format or degree of difficulty. No one ever asks you in later life how you did on your SAT IIs.

The ACT is a quasi-legitimate alternative to the SATs. Nobody seems to know where it came from or who started it or why. Nobody even knows what ACT stands for. Scores on the ACT run from 1 to 36, leaving open the dangerous possibility of getting a single-digit score. Luckily, as with the SAT IIs, virtually no one will ask you about your ACT scores in later life. In any case, revealing your ACT score ("Thanks for asking, I got a 22") is like telling someone the temperature in Celsius: there is no frame of reference; they won't get it.

## How Fair Are the SATs?

They really aren't very fair at all. For years, the questions were directed at the sensibilities of white upper-middle-class teenagers, leaving those from lower socioeconomic classes without much of a chance. For example, here's this question from the 1998 test:

> Q. Dad, this Passat's _____ is really _____.
>    A. acceleration . . . sketchy
>    B. leather . . . Naugahyde
>    C. gas mileage . . . earth unfriendly
>    D. finish . . . finicky

Or, going way back, this one from 1966:

> Q. After Labor Day, _____ is not very _____.
>    A. madras . . . appropriate
>    B. the Martha's Vineyard ferry . . . crowded
>    C. the Yale-Harvard game . . . far away
>    D. the bond market . . . active

As you can see, the questions tended to tilt toward the interests of a very small but powerful segment of society. However, as college became a reality for more and more graduating high school seniors from all economic classes, the bias of the SATs had to change. And change it has, as evidenced by this question from the 2003 test:

> Q. Yo, dog, getcha _____ on the _____!
>    A. ass . . . dance floor
>    B. dog . . . dog pile
>    C. South Side . . . upside
>    D. clothes off . . . double

No doubt, more work needs to be done, but fairness has never been an SAT strong point, so tell your child to get over it. Everyone's taking the same test.

## Strategies for Success

Since any hopes for a decent life hinge on the SATs, it's a good idea to figure out how to do well on them. There are three basic

strategies that the student can employ, albeit with a great deal of
help and even interference from you:

**1. Do-it-yourself vocabulary building at home.** This in-
volves getting a list of thousands of vocabulary words that have
been, or might be, used on SAT verbal sections and going over
them every day for several years leading up to the test. An ambitious parent's goal would be to have the child recite the words
and their meanings in the same scary way (except, if at all possible, without the facial tics and pooping in the pants) those fi-
nalists in the National Spelling Bee recall and correctly spell
words that no one has ever heard of. There are two good ways to
achieve this sublime, half-crazy level of perfection.

—Make your child stand by your side, and every time he defines a word properly you feed him a fish from a small pail at your
feet.

—Pretend the vocab words are a new foreign language you all
must master. One fun exercise is to use as many of the words as
you can around the dinner table:

"This is a savory meal of viands, Mom, but a bit scanty."

"I laud you for your lament. I'd be more lavish if I could kindle
your labyrinth."

"You're meandering again into the problematic."

"Such quiescent heterodox, you gratuitous, detrimental plight."

And so on.

**2. Hire a tutor.** Plenty of tutors are available for the math or
verbal sections, or both, of the SAT. All make extravagant claims
but, according to the National Association of Bright-but-Bored
Moms Who've Become SAT Tutors, the score of the average child
taking such a course indeed rises 200, 300, or even 400 points.
There have even been several cases of a tutored student scoring
slightly above 2400 in the combined scores, a truly remarkable
achievement. A tutor's job is not to help the student learn but to
teach how to outfox the people who draw up the test. They do
this by studying many years worth of tests and ferreting out ten-
dencies or patterns in the questions and answers. For example,
they've found that any time the word "red" appears in a question, the answer is C. Mention of a nocturnal hunting mammal

almost always means the answer is A. The words "but," "not," "however," and "therefore" are not to be lightly regarded. The word "shucks" can usually be ignored, whether used as a verb or an interjection. Math problems involving circles that intersect never have C or A as an answer. How else will your child (and you) learn such important facts and gain an advantage in the overall scheme of things unless you engage a tutor?

**3. Cheat.** Why should prospective Division I football and basketball players have all the fun? There are dozens of ways to cheat on the SATs, many of them virtually undetectable. The best way: Spend $100 and have someone smarter take the test! What could be simpler? And compare that cost to the $750 or $1,000 or even more that a tutor charges. Save that money for later, when you'll need to send expensive boxes of perfectly ripened grapefruits and pears to admissions officers.

## Extra Time

If your child could use extra time in taking the SATs, then by all means claim "special needs" status. This incredibly unfair advantage was once handed out only to legitimate qualifiers, like kids with dyslexia or felony convictions. But now all sorts of conditions will qualify your son or daughter for those precious extra minutes. Some recent examples of claims that were granted:

—Applicant has trouble concentrating in rooms where trees with swaying branches are visible through the windows.

—Applicant given to embarrassing sneezing fits that affect self-esteem.

—Applicant "just doesn't get" some of the questions on standardized tests.

—If a friend jumps off the Brooklyn Bridge, applicant will do so as well.

It's worth noting that if a student is given extra time on the test, prospective colleges will be so informed by an asterisk that indicates "nonstandard administration." Another asterisk will be added if the applicant is the first one off the Brooklyn Bridge.

## Product Placement in the New SAT

One disturbing trend in recent years has been the College Board's willingness to allow commercial sponsors a place within test questions. For a fee of forty thousand dollars, a company can acquire a spot in either a math or verbal question ("Contrary to her customary _____ behavior, Betty began leaving parties early to enjoy a Winston cigarette"), while seventy-five thousand will get a place as the correct answer in one of the multiple-choice possibilities:

> Q.  Excited and unafraid, the _____ child examined the candy-bearing stranger with bright-eyed curiosity.
>     A.  apathetic
>     B.  hungry-for-a-Snickers
>     C.  hesitant
>     D.  timorous

The latest word is that the SAT Board is considering offers in the millions of dollars for selling off the naming rights to the entire test. Among the possible new names are the Mountain Dew SATs, the Nike SATs, and the Grand Theft Auto SATs.

## The SAT Itself

As stated earlier, the big test now has three parts: math, verbal, and writing sample. The verbal section further breaks down into two sections: critical reading and sentence completion. Let's take a look at these last two to begin with.

### Critical Reading

Many colleges believe that their incoming freshmen should be able to read and understand at least several consecutive sentences in English, and that is what this part of the SAT was designed to ascertain. It consists of passages of text, roughly 500–800 words long, followed by a series of seemingly unrelated questions. The passages should not be confused with pleasure reading. There should be no lingering over well-turned phrases or chuckling aloud at humorous descriptions. Students taking the test need to remember that they are not relaxing by a lake on a summer afternoon, *they are taking the SATs!* Their future is very much at stake. They need to read, answer the questions, and move on. While it's true that many of the passages on the actual SATs have to do with hydroponic farming and the mating habits of insects, students should be prepared for a variety of subjects. What follows for your review (and don't hesitate to share it with your child) is an actual passage and questions taken from a recent test:

Reading Test #1. Questions 1–3 are based on the passage below.

When at last she felt perfectly satisfied with them, she said one morning: "Come along, children. Follow me." Before you could wink an eyelash Jack, Kack, Lack, Mack, Nack, Ouack, Pack, and Quack fell into line, just as they had been taught. Mrs. Mallard led the way into the water and they swam behind her to the opposite bank.

There they waded ashore and waddled along till they came to the highway.

Mrs. Mallard stepped out to cross the road. "Honk, honk!" went the horns on the speeding cars. "Qua-a-ack!" went Mrs. Mallard as she tumbled back again. "Quack! Quack! Quack! Quack!" went Jack, Kack, Lack, Mack, Nack, Ouack, Pack, and Quack, just as loud as their little quackers could quack. The cars kept speeding by and honking, and Mrs. Mallard and the ducklings kept right on quack-quack-quacking.

1. Just before this passage begins, the oldest duckling was killed by a horrible little man with a hammer. This duckling's name was
   A. Snack
   B. Wack
   C. Iak
   D. Shaq

2. Where is Mr. Mallard?
    A. No longer in the picture
    B. Playing cards with the boys
    C. Hangin' with a certain Ms. Merganser
    D. Mrs. Mallard is not positive who the father is

3. Why are the ducks crossing the road?
    A. Someone said something about food
    B. No reason—they're a bunch of stupid ducks
    C. They're looking for Mr. Mallard
    D. They heard about the chickens doing it

## Sentence Completion

Here, students are provided with a choice of words to best complete a sentence. Sometimes more than one answer seems correct, and, indeed, sometimes more than one answer is acceptable. In a few rare cases, all the answers are actually correct. Here are a few samples of the sorts of questions you'll find in this section of the verbal:

1. Most Americans would agree that Richard Nixon was a(n) _____ president.
    A. crispy
    B. ancillary
    C. Korean
    D. minute

2. The average consumer ranks _____ as the favorite of all automobile options.
    A. cupholders large enough to hold a Big Gulp
    B. tiny blue lights on the windshield washers
    C. $10,000 worth of fried food
    D. license plates bordered by fake chains

3. Running home to see his mommy, the little crybaby was _____ when the other kids in the neighborhood _____ his mittens.
    A. flustrated . . . secreted
    B. apoplectic . . . ignited

C. vengeful . . . slashed

D. allowed extra time on his SATs . . . let a St. Bernard drool on

## Why the Analogies Were Dropped

The reason is so simple that test takers in the past may want to slap themselves for not having spotted it. Are you ready?

Take a good look at this analogy taken from an actual test given in 1982:

Q. Apple is to orchard as ------ is to ------ -----.

A. egg . . . carton

B. smoke . . . chimney

C. orange . . . orange grove

D. tree . . . forest

Can you see why the correct answer is C? Simply go back and count the number of dashes in the question. It's as simple as that. Once word got out, the folks in Princeton had no choice but to come up with something different.

## Writing Section

This fancy new piece in the SAT puzzle was added in the 2004–05 school year because . . . well, really for no reason at all, at least not one that is evident. Perhaps colleges wanted to see if students could string a few coherent sentences together without a parent or advisor literally guiding the pencil for them. Perhaps it grew out of an altruistic impulse on the part of the College Board to employ thousands of scuffling freelance writers, down-on-their-luck poets, and English teachers on probation for sexual shenanigans as readers and graders of this new section. Or maybe the Board just wanted to see what would happen if performances were not graded objectively but rather based on the prejudices, political philosophies, and whims of the judges. Whatever the reason, the writing section is here and your child will need to prepare for it.

It is composed of two sections:

## Multiple Choice Questions

### Identifying Sentence Errors

Here the student will find sentences with several of the words italicized. The trick is to find the italicized part that is somehow not up to the standards of the rest of the sentence. To get your child to pay attention here, it might be helpful for you to remind him or her of the drawings in *Highlights* magazine in which the young reader was asked to find the things that were "wrong" in the picture (such as bricks coming out of a garden hose). Here's a typical sentence from an actual test:

> Academicians *believe* that *Abbott and Costello* and
>               A                  B
> *Laurel and Hitler* have much to teach the new generation
>        C
> of *college-bound* students. *No error*.
>       D               E

If you believe you've spotted the error, enter the letter on the answer sheet and quickly move along to the next challenge.

### Improving Sentences

In this section, students will find a test sentence that is not necessarily incorrect but that can nonetheless be improved. See if you can spot the sentence improving answer from the choices below:

> For your hard work, here's a check for $120.
>     A. For your hard work, here's a kick in the pants.
>     B. For your hard work, here's a check for $17,000.
>     C. For your hard work, here's a copy of the prayer we'll say for you in church on Sunday.
>     D. For your hard work, here's a piece of dog doo.

*Improving Paragraphs*

This part of the new SAT writing section is so brutally boring and unrelated to anything approaching real life that even I, who is being paid to put this guide together, cannot bring myself to discuss it or help you or your child prepare for it.

## *The Essay*

This new section of the SAT is interesting primarily because it requires a good amount of writing at a time when high school students, as a whole, have never had worse handwriting skills. This is not the students' fault, of course. No one teaches good handwriting any more; indeed, no teacher has graded for penmanship since 1966. Students aren't even taught how to hold a pencil. They do most of their writing on computer screens anyway so perhaps, the thinking goes, it doesn't matter all that much.

*Except now.*

*On the most important test they'll ever take.*

Students are given twenty-five minutes to write on an assigned topic. If they decide to write on another topic or on essentially no topic at all, well, there are plenty of colleges that will think that's pretty cool. In any event, here's a sample taken from the 2005 test:

Think carefully about the issue presented in the following excerpt:

Money is the best motivation and reward for one's achievements. Expecting happiness and fulfillment is not realistic and it can lead to disappointment and frustration. If we want to be happy in what we do in life, we should seek achievement for the sake of winning wealth and fame. The personal satisfaction of a job well done is strictly for the birds.

**Assignment:** *Everyone loves money. Plan and write an essay in which you express your own feelings about money—coins, folding cash (fins, sawbucks, double sawbucks, Franklins, etc.), bullion, foreign currency, lucre, loot, pelf, cheese, stink, bread, cabbage, celery—the look of it, the smell of it, the handsome heft of it in*

*pocket or purse. Support your observations with vignettes and*
*lively anecdotes taken from your own experience or from popular*
*TV shows or commercials.*

As it turned out, the grading for this particular essay broke
pretty much along alphabetical lines, with students with last
names ending in A–D receiving a 6 (the highest score), names
ending E–H receiving a 5, and so on. That's nothing to count
on, however, and the College Board is sure to come up with a
new grading twist every year. Although I haven't had a lot of
time yet to devise strategies for parents in this area, I do recommend writing the word ESSAY in large block letters on in-
dex cards and putting them up on the kitchen bulletin board,
refrigerator, bedroom mirror, and other key spots around the
house. I hope to come up with some better ideas in future edi-
tions of this book.

## Mathematics

The thing about math is your answer is either right or it's wrong,
either you are a genius or you suck. Some students are gifted at
math, but neither they nor their parents buy books like this. They
don't need advice. They've got the wind at their backs, the numbers lined up neatly in their minds, the colleges sending them
recruitment letters with full-ride scholarships and promises of
unlimited drugs and sex. And why is all this happening? Basically
because when most of us look at home plate, we think, "baseball,"
and when they look at home plate, they think, "pentagonal plain";
when the word "cone" is mentioned, we think of vanilla ice cream
with rainbow sprinkles and they think of hard-to-remember formulae for volume and area; and when we hear the word "mean,"
we think of our fifth-grade teacher, Miss Griswold, and they think
of medians, modes, averages, and all those "in the middle" math
words that are similar but apparently not identical.

The SAT math section includes multiple choice questions and
something new called Student-Produced Responses. It's only by
going over problems like these repeatedly that your child will

begin to feel confident with his or her math skills. There should be some comfort taken by both of you from the knowledge that none of this nonsense will ever again matter. At all. Ever.

## Standard Multiple Choice

Q. There are two roads between London and Edinburgh. If Frank takes the high road and Amber takes the low road, who will get to Scotland "afore" the other?
   A. Frank
   B. Amber
   C. They will arrive at the same time
   D. Both will be greatly delayed or never arrive at all
   E. Haggis
   F. Let's take a pass and move on to the next question, shall we?

Q. If x equals 7 and y equals 3, what does z equal, in laymen's terms?
   A. 10
   B. 4
   C. 21
   D. 73
   E. all of the above

Q. A Pyramid, a Cube, and a Cylinder walk into a bar. The Pyramid says to the bartender, "I'd like to buy a drink for me and my two friends." The bartender looks at the three of them and says, _____.
   A. "I'd love to, but this is a two-dimensional joint."
   B. "Did you realize that your friend the Sphere rolled out of here at about 2 a.m. this morning?"
   C. "No way, it looks like you've already had your volume."
   D. "Sure. On the rocks for you, Cube?"

## Student-Produced Responses

Here is where the SATs in effect leave the student alone on a desert island with only a safety pin and a book of matches. There are no multiple choices to choose from in this section, no comforting patterns that halfway provide alert students with the correct answers. Instead, by placing a dot or a line on a graph (or something like that), the student is supposed to answer a question like: "What will happen to the train and all the passengers when the railroad tracks narrow and finally come together at the horizon?"

In this section, it is possible for students to be so wrong with their answers that they bring down not only this section, but the two verbal sections as well.

## Final Tips on Taking the SAT

There are some general procedures that your child should consider.

—Serious candidates for top colleges do not go to the special midnight SAT, at which students dress up as characters from *Ferris Bueller's Day Off* and *The Breakfast Club* and sing and act out the test directions and even some of the questions.
—The SAT is considering giving an extra hundred points to the first student to finish the test at each of the testing centers. Check and find out if this is the case. If it is, it's probably worth racing through the material as quickly as you can.
—Answer first the questions to which you know the answers. If you arrive at the end of the section without having filled out a single answer, let's face it, you're totally screwed.
—Wrong answers hurt you more than nonanswers, but you must weigh how confident you feel. If you feel 70 percent confident on a given answer, then go ahead and fill it in. Anywhere from 64 to 69 percent, you'll have to think it through, but probably answer it. If you're at 63 percent down to 54 or 55 percent, it's time to consult the Magic 8-Ball key chain you brought along (and hope it doesn't keep advising to "Try Again Later").

—On questions for which two or more answers are clearly correct, simply fill in all the bubbles and draw a small screaming monkey on the test sheet next to the question.

—Remember that the math formulae you learned in high school are not used on the SAT. You must employ the new ones that you will be expected to use in college.

—Don't get involved in side issues. If a sentence-completion question seems to indicate that ex–White Sox star Harold Baines should be in the Baseball Hall of Fame, and you disagree, now is not the time to dash off notes to officials in Princeton and Cooperstown.

—Keep in mind that if you don't answer any of the questions, your money will be cheerfully refunded.

At college fairs, some schools will give seniors the chance to
knock down a pyramid of milk bottles with a spongy old softball.
If they knock them down, they are admitted with the incoming
freshman class.

# 4

# Narrowing
# the Choice

## Strategies for Success

Although some "can't-make-up-their-mind" high-school seniors
have apparently come close, it's really not practical to apply to
every college in America. Just the cost of the application fees
alone is more than most families would feel comfortable spend-
ing. If there are, say, two thousand four-year colleges in the country, and the average application fee is $50, that's $100,000 right
there. Then there'd be another $800 or so for postage, not to
mention the hassle of all those campus visits, interviews, and essays. Such an undertaking also places an unfair burden on those
expected to provide recommendations for the applicant. After all,
what busy professional wants to spend his or her evenings thinking up two thousand different ways of saying "average"?

Our advice, therefore, is to assess your child's capabilities and
career to date and then narrow his or her choices to a handful of
appropriate schools. This chapter is designed to help you do just
that.

## Evaluating Your Child

To know what sort of college your child should attend, you first need to know your child. What does he like to do? In what circumstances is he most comfortable? What sorts of friends does he enjoy most? What is his name? It's only after answering questions like this that you can begin pushing your child toward the school of your choice.

One way to get this process started is to have your child compose a list of impressions of his or her high school career. Having such a document, seeing in black and white your child's likes, dislikes, fears, obsessions, urges, appetites, and addictions will help you determine who your child is and what direction might be advisable for the next four years. Here's the beginning of a typical list written by a female high school senior from Roanoke, Virginia:

*Who I Honestly Am (Hello, Mom)*
1. First of all, I'M LIKE SO NOT DOING THIS LIST ON MY OWN!!! I mean OMG it's so totally not my idea!! Yeah. Well. So here we go.
2. In Biology I like to sit behind Ross the big wrestler so I can just sort of hide out and take it easy.
3. The teachers in my high school are like so unimpressive and weird. I think the teachers in college will be more impressive because they must be smarter to be teaching in college, plus I don't think they really care what you do out of class or in the corridors. I'm not sure if there even are corridors in college.
4. I don't really get politics or religion. They're both important and I know I should try harder, but the people into them in school are just so off on their own. I do believe that Martin Luther King was a great man and we should pay attention to what he said and all.
5. I hate cold weather. I like pictures of snow and the idea of being out in the snow, but every time I try I just get so cold to the bone that I have to go inside. I hate spiders and flies and ants, too, and flying. And I really hate mushrooms and Bugles . . .

And so, eventually, by such examination will the college applicant and the parent come up with an idea of what you are both looking for in a college.

## A Survey of College Types

Once you have determined who your child is, where, exactly, should you push him or her into college? To get you started, remember that colleges and universities in the United States conveniently break down into several broad categories. There are some schools that manage to tightrope-walk between two classifications, but most don't. In fact, most can really be summed up in a sentence or two. Here are the main examples:

**The Faceless Diploma Mill.** You'll find here at least twenty-five thousand students on campus, and sometimes many more. Students live in gigantic high-rise dorms that are like small cities, with crime, poverty, illiteracy, transportation issues, lots of people who speak little or no English, and others who are clearly off their meds. The football stadium is huge, making it perfect for some of the larger survey courses. Graduation Day is an insanely overcrowded joke. Campus police carry guns and aren't shy about using them.

**The Extended Prep School.** These are small liberal-arts colleges, usually located in the Northeast, where skiing, squash, blond good looks, and effective layering are given inordinate emphasis. After graduation, students continue living together in apartments in Back Bay or Manhattan, keeping the prep-school dream alive until they can begin marrying each other, having little blond children, and beginning the process all over again.

**The Crazy Religious School.** Often named after a person, but may also have the name of the religion, or similar words ("Bible," "Theological," "Chiropractic," etc.) right up there in the name of the school. Every few years, a coed poses for *Playboy* and all hell breaks loose.

**The Hippie School.** No grading, no real studying, and everything's organic and sustainable, from the hemp clothing on the students to the shrubbery served in the dining hall. Athletic letters are awarded for Hacky Sack and cartwheels. School holidays granted for especially nice snowfalls.

**The Very Expensive Mediocre School.** Popular in recent years as parents who cannot get their children into top colleges at least want them to go someplace that's incredibly expensive. Easily identifiable by the fact that ten years ago, basically anyone who wanted to go could get in, but now they're fairly competitive (but not competitive enough to keep your child out if you're willing to pay the full freight).

**The Loser School with the Huge Car-window Decal.** Generally speaking, there is an inverse relationship between the quality of the college and the size of its decal. The largest decals are used by schools that believe clever branding (large decals, coffee mugs, big foam "We're No. 1" fingers, etc.) is a budget-smart alternative to finding and paying top faculty.

**Schools with Funny Names.** Like having an embarrassing middle name, graduates from these places must live down the name of their school for the rest of their lives. Indiana of Pennsylvania is one silly example, as are Harvey Mudd, Slippery Rock, Dropsie, Rust, and Oklahoma Panhandle State College of Agriculture & Applied Sciences (try fitting that one on a sweatshirt).

## The Overseas Option

Students who really don't want to have anything more to do with their parents, families, or hometown honeys should recognize they have the option of attending a school overseas. This also works for parents who wish to position a child as far away from home as possible without actually being charged with abandonment.

There are many good schools in other countries, but quite a few that are roughly on a par with your local 7-Eleven in their ability to educate your child. As you scan through the catalogs and Web sites for overseas schools, here are some things to consider:

—A British accent, even a very poor one acquired during a few semesters abroad, will guarantee your child a good job as a phone receptionist at virtually any New York public relations agency. Even just the frequent use of several key British words such as "dodgy" or "suss" can secure such a position.

—The educational experience at Oxbridge includes punting on the Cam. At no school in America is it possible to punt on the Cam. In fact, even in England no one knows for sure what punting on the Cam means. (And, by the way, "Oxbridge" is a word used to denote both Oxford and Cambridge. It might be fun if some schools in the States did the same, such as Pepperdine and Alcorn State or Butler and Morehead State.)

—It's easy to get into the universities in Central Asia, but the food in the cafeterias is not the greatest and the bus rides along the Silk Road to other schools for mixers and such can be long and tedious if not interrupted by earthquakes or America-hating kidnappers.

—There is a college in Romania called Harvud. It's not easy to get to, and it's not going to win any awards for academic excellence, but think about it.

## Narrowing the Choice

Despite all your efforts, your child will eventually narrow his or her choices by using rumor; hearsay; cues picked up from movies, popular music, and bumper stickers; and where cool friends are going. Still, the winnowing process has begun. Now it's time to take a serious look at the fifteen or twenty schools still under consideration. Colleges can be classified in three main categories of selectivity: Astonishingly Demanding (AD), Excessively Demanding (ED), and Surprisingly Demanding (SD). You should make sure that your child has several schools from each category on his or her list (and maybe the phone number of the local armed forces recruiting office, just in case). With the list in hand, let's begin our study of each school's pros and cons. There are several main ways in which this can be done before you commit to visiting the school itself.

## E-mail Solicitations

This is usually your child's first contact with many schools. The e-mails seem to be personally addressed ("We're looking for curious students just like you, Ned," it might say in the subject line), but they're just part of a massive, computer-generated mailing to anyone who has taken a PSAT, rented a movie at Blockbuster, or bought Skittles from a vending machine. Considering that the first wave of these e-mails go to high school sophomores, they can have a surprisingly desperate tone ("We only have one brochure left, Julie!!!" or "I'm ready to jump off this ledge, Sam!") or strike an inappropriate theme ("Add inches to your johnson, Jackson!"). Needless to say, none of the schools that engage in blanket e-mailing can truly be considered "top."

## College Brochures, Viewbooks, and Web Sites

The college brochure, viewbook, and Web site will quickly become familiar parts of the application process, and it won't take long before you notice a certain squishy sameness as you turn from one to the next. Here's a grassy quad scattered with golden October leaves, there's a minority person looking closely at a beaker in a science lab, here's a handsome jock kicking a soccer ball, there's a multicultural group laughing as a chocolate lab catches a Frisbee. All of which prompts me to ask: "Would it be so wrong for a brochure or Web site to actually show the applicant what the school is really like?"

Even the language employed by the colleges is suspect. Certain words and phrases you'll see all the time may seem innocuous enough, or even inviting, but to the experienced eye they can mean something completely different. Make sure you don't get taken in by them. Here's what they really mean:

"World-Class" = Average.

"All-Season Fun" = Brutal, dark winters that last until May.

"City Excitement" = Dangerous, possibly even deadly, after dark.

"Undiscovered Gem" = Semiprecious.

"Active Lifestyle" = Unattractively muscular students of both genders wear hiking boots and shorts all year round.

"Diverse" = Not very diverse.

The Web sites and viewbooks are touted as good sources for specific information about the school. My suggestion is that you read them in the same way you'd read a movie review written by the people who'd invested all their money in the movie.

# The College Fair

Although there is always the danger that your child will choose a college based on the quality of the pencils given away at these events, college fairs present a good opportunity to speak to a school's traveling representatives. Dozens of colleges set up booths, often in a local hotel conference center or high school gym, and hand out stacks of printed information. There is usually cotton candy and fried dough available to eat, sometimes corn on the cob and turkey drumsticks. Some schools will give seniors the chance to knock down a pyramid of milk bottles with a spongy old softball. If they knock them down, they are automatically admitted with the incoming freshman class. Other schools present variations on this theme, with admission guaranteed if seniors can hook a wooden fish in a tank of water, burst a balloon with water from a squirt gun, toss a wooden ring around a rolled-up "diploma," or guess the weight of the school mascot. Tell your child not to get too excited, though. These games are much harder than they look.

The fairs are fun, but they can also lead to bad decision making. As I mentioned earlier, some schools hand out very handsome mechanical pencils or tell impressionable high schoolers that taking and wearing a college's T-shirt represents a commitment to go to that school. You may not think your boy or girl can be so easily misled, but I have documented stories of kids who go to a fair only to come back home in tears having decided on a college because its school colors were "awesome," the booth was giving away packages of sunflower seeds, or the mascot said something funny.

My advice: let the kids go to the fair, but always keep in mind that the traveling representatives of the colleges have much more experience in the ways of the world than a typical high school senior does. Tell them to enjoy themselves, but not to sign anything.

## Books and Periodicals

First of all, thank you for buying this book—assuming you did buy it and didn't just borrow it from someone else or check it out of the library, or that you're not just standing there in the bookstore, or, even worse, seated in one of those comfortable armchairs, *reading for free!* What the hell is wrong with you? Doesn't it make you at all uncomfortable, pissing away the afternoon like that while others are out accomplishing things, even if it's just washing the car or dropping stuff off in the used-clothing bin in the strip-mall parking lot? And don't you feel guilty, not paying for something that someone worked very hard on, someone with children in school, with bills to pay and fairly serious gambling debts to make good on? I've always gone to Barnes & Noble and wondered, "Who are these people in the armchairs, anyway?" Now I know. Thank you. Now I know.

Secondly, you've probably noticed all the other books crowding the shelves in the "College Preparation" section of the bookstore. There are the SAT prep books, of course, and the big books with profiles of hundreds of colleges written by people who haven't visited the campuses since Livingston Taylor was coming on strong. There are college-profile books written by gangs of students or former students with huge agendas and axes to grind, exposés penned by ungrateful former admissions-office deans, and guides to the millions of dollars in grants available to you if only your daughter were a baton twirling descendent of the Hodge family of Nevada, or your son the son of a victim of the huge River Rouge gas explosion of 1974.

You might also have noticed the number of books with the word "Ivy" in the title. There's *The Ivy Enigma,* for example, or *The View from the Ivy Tower*. There's *Chicken Soup for the Pro-*

*spective Ivy Leaguer's Parent* and *Harry Potter and the Labyrinth of the Ivy Application.* All are shamelessly trying to cash in on even the faintest relationship with one of the elite Ivy League colleges. In truth, there are only a small handful of books that are really worth buying and using for your child's college-admissions effort. They are:

*Smashing Your Way into College* by Caz Cazminski. A useful and memorable how-to on the use of brute force and threats of violence to get your child into a top school.

*I Married a Dean of Admissions* by Eleanor Lupid-Stone. A provocative inside look at the admissions process from across the breakfast table. With a fascinating anecdote on the role really good marmalade played in winning one man's heart.

*Mascot of Steel* by Nathaniel Fletycher. How a resourceful high school cheerleader turned his grandfather's old raccoon coat into admissions gold. Later surfaced as a Rob Schneider box-office dud.

*Safety Schools* by Hanford Brown. Never mind the top colleges for once, how about a guide to the schools that everyone can get into? Profusely illustrated, with letters of acceptance included.

## College Ranking Systems

Although college administrators won't admit it, the ranking systems used by *U.S. News & World Report* and other publications are completely accurate. The rankings are compiled by hard-working unpaid editorial interns who learn in a very short time how to combine a vast array of statistical information with just enough journalistic swagger to pull the whole thing off. Is Cal Tech really better than MIT? Could Johns Hopkins be that far ahead of Brown? Well, my friend, prove that they aren't.

That said, the rankings very rarely deal with the aspects of college life that are most important to the greatest number of potential undergraduates. Who cares how many students graduate within six years of matriculation, or what percentage of teachers are part-time instructors? What your child wants to know is how far it is to the nearest ESPN Zone and whether cinnamon Pop-Tarts are served at breakfast, lunch, and dinner. Median SAT scores are one thing, but how about high SAT scores from students who are also cute and rich with nice cars and summer homes?

My suggestion is that you accept the findings of the established rankings, but then add your own categories and rerank according to your own child's (or your own) needs, desires, and dislikes. Some of the pluses and minuses you might consider researching are:

—Number of courses taught by funny professors.

—Basketball crowds consisting of thousands of students all wearing the same-colored shirts, yelling the same cheers, and making the same gestures.

—Campus buildings designed to look like Independence Hall in Philadelphia.

—Ample and convenient parking for parents when they come to visit. Also, easy on and off from nearby interstate highway.

—Number of nice, polite, well-adjusted kids in the student population who send thank-you notes after you've taken them out to dinner or had them stay for an overnight.

## The Consultant

Like a cocksure, hectoring whirlwind, the high-priced consultant has blown onto the college-admission scene and helped turn a once reasonably civilized procedure into a me-first blood sport. The modern consultant comes in many different forms, all of them expensive. Those at the head of the game tend to be combative thirtyish females—rail-thin top-college grads living on nail polish fumes and vodka. They claim near perfection in getting clients into what one enigmatically calls "schools of choice."

The consultant's level of participation in your child's life depends on how much you pay her. Those at the very high end will cook for the family and provide neck massages and air miles. Those at the low end offer refrigerator magnets. At whatever level, the consultant's job is to slap your child around and fictionalize his or her academic career and extracurricular activities in a way that even normally astute college-admissions committees will accept as true.

In recent years, consultants have become more and more specialized, limiting their efforts to tennis players, science students, chess wizards, and the like. There is even a consultant in New York City who works only with salutatorians, and another who has made a career of taking one–time Cub Scouts and altar boys, outfitting them with outlandish recovered memories, and turning them into incoming Ivy League freshmen.

My advice is to find an admissions officer at a top college who moonlights as a consultant, hire her, and then apply to the college she works for.

---

### Free Advice from College Consultants

As I researched *How to Get a Monkey into Harvard*, I visited with some of the sought after consultants in America and refused to leave until they gave me one or more gems of advice for your child:

"Take courses that are too hard for you and get A's in them. If you're interested in politics, run for mayor. English? Publish a best-selling novel. Does your school have a model UN team? Learn an obscure African dialect and ask for aid."

"Write your essay on the back of an envelope containing $200,000."

"Take a year or two off to live at the school you're interested in; stay in a dorm, eat in the dining hall, try out for a team, attend classes, fall in love and break up and then fall in love again. Only then will you know whether the school is the right one for you."

"Are you a jock? Then learn to speak in jock clichés. Athletic departments are favorably disposed toward an applicant who says he wants to play 'one game at a time' or likes to 'leave my game on the field.' And if you can toss in a reassuring classic, like 'My future is definitely ahead of me,' you are virtually assured of admission."

"Some colleges are experimenting with super-early admissions, which allows you to apply in the middle of your freshman year in high school. If you can take an AP course or two during your seventh- and eighth-grade summers, I heartily recommend this course of action. You'll be left with three years for nothing but fun."

On organized campus tours, there's always one parent who tries to be funny and for some reason tries to ingratiate himself with the student guide. Don't be that person. The guide cannot help your child get into the school.

# 5

# Campus Visit
# and Interview

## The Visit

"I always looked forward to visiting colleges with my son," writes a Missouri mom. "I pictured it in fall, the two of us driving along country roads, strolling the campuses, poking our heads into classrooms—and in the process really getting to *know* each other, finding out what he feels about things, what his hopes are for the future, what makes him tick. But then as we traveled along together, and I asked him questions and, frankly, did far, far more than my fair share of keeping the conversation going, it hit me: He doesn't tick at all. He eats and sleeps and says 'Yeah.' For all he cared, we could have been visiting cheese factories. I saw more clearly than ever that this whole college-admissions process was in my hands."

Indeed, going on campus visits is one of the best ways you can assure yourself that your child will end up at a college of your choosing. Using the advice in Chapter Four and your own influence, you narrowed the choices down to twenty schools or so, but

now you can realistically visit no more than ten of them, probably fewer. Is your child going to be the one to map out a coordi-
nated plan of attack and make meal arrangements and motel
reservations? Hardly. All you have to do at this point is propose
a tour and your child will most likely go along with it, probably
with a sense of relief that someone else is willing to do all the
work. (Have him print out directions from mapquest.com if he
claims that he wants to feel involved.)

The main thing for you to understand as a parent at this stage
of the game is that although you've literally spent years meticu-
lously laying out all the groundwork for these visits, your child's
decision will come as the result of a snap judgment—the same
sort of natural instinct that allows birds and fish to suddenly veer
away from danger and toward safety. As you both step out of the
car and onto an actual campus, the whole "going to college thing"
will suddenly become very real to your high schooler. It's no
longer an abstraction of random brochures and Web sites and
coaching from you—instead it's:

"Oh my God, this place sucks!"

"Well, you really haven't seen any of it yet."

"I wouldn't be caught dead here in a million years."

"Why not?"

"Because it's [a look of disgust that you could even conceiv-
ably ask such a question] . . . *bad*."

And you will have a noticeably sullen companion for the re-
mainder of your visit.

Fortunately, not every campus you've picked out will
elicit this response. The same radar that can detect a "sucky"
school in thirty seconds can perform the same trick with a
good one.

"Oh my God, this place is great!"

"Well, you really haven't seen any of it yet."

"Can we get a sweatshirt?"

"Well . . . sure!"

And now the campus visit, and interview, can proceed as
planned.

> ### The Best Time to Visit
>
> Big partying weekends are always fun. If you can tuck your little one into bed at a reasonable hour, you'll still be able to get over to frater- nity row for live music, free beer, and some unbeatable vicarious thrills. Who knows—you may even be able to hook up with another visiting parent who's secretly yearning to make up for lost opportuni- ties during his or her own college days!

# The Information Session

The information session is an excellent time for you and your child to get a good look at the other students who are interested in going to a particular school, and, of course, for you to get a look at their parents. While a perky young admissions officer stands in the front of the room and chirps on and on about class size, meal plans, and the like, you can use the time to check out the competition (especially if you've been smart enough to take a seat toward the rear). Here's a mop-haired boy nodding off while his mother furiously scribbles notes in a loose-leaf binder; there's the blazer-clad dad who will soon jump up and, in ask- ing a question, let everyone know where he went to college. Here's a much older couple (grandparents? Albatross parents?) sitting a significant distance away from their inattentive young charge; there's a no-nonsense couple who've apparently decided to dispense with all pretense and have left their child at home. All in all, are these people with whom you can feel comfortable? Do they speak well? Are they wearing good shoes? Do their children pose a significant threat to your own child's wavering sense of self-worth? Such are the questions to answer in your own loose-leaf binder.

You will note that parents ask 95 percent of the questions at these information sessions. If you decide to ask one or two, you should try to make sure they cast you in a positive light in the eyes of the perky admissions officer (after all, she may be the one who eventually decides your child's fate) and, if possible, stir envy among the other parents. You will know you've succeeded if some sitting up in front crane their necks to see who's asking the question. Remember: at this point in the process, no one knows who you are, so you don't even have to pose a truthful question. Some examples:

—In arriving at its decision, will the admissions committee consider something nontraditional like my daughter's architecture portfolio?

—If a student comes into the college already fluent in Arabic and Chinese, what sort of further advancement in these languages is possible here?

—Does the admissions office have someone who specializes in dealing with the problems of heavily recruited, Olympics-level athletes?

## Campus Tour: The Parent's Role

Everyone needs to keep in mind that this whole college-admissions process is as much about you as it is about your child, if not more so. It's your transition, too—your change of life. You have wants and needs that deserve to be addressed. Even so, there are certain guidelines that you should probably follow—basic rules you should remember—as you make your way around campus with your child.

—No one wants to hear about your own memories of college life. No one cares about the Moody Blues.

—Unless you are touring a Mormon or Baptist school or service academy, there is no such thing as "inappropriate" dress on a college campus, so don't use that word as you plead against your daughter's purple and black Goth getup.

—On organized campus tours, there's always one parent who tries to be funny and for some reason tries to ingratiate himself with the student guide. Don't be that person. The guide cannot help your child get into the school.

—Are you a racist, or do you feel uncomfortable in the presence of those who are not just like you? If so, a top-college campus may prove to be a challenge. Again, don't joke about it or nervously act out broad racial stereotypes. Some may not "get" that you're just being funny.

## Some Concerns to Address During Your Campus Visit

If you're seeing a school for the first time, or even if you think you know it well, there are all sorts of things to watch for as you visit the campus. Don't be afraid to ask as many questions as you need to in order to feel comfortable. All college employees are basically being paid to answer your questions, be they admissions officials, professors, coaches, campus police, clergy, or buildings-and-grounds personnel. It can be a real time-saver, at least for you, if you can buttonhole one person and get him or her to answer all of your queries. After posing more than a few myself during my research, I've come up with the following lists that you may find useful:

### Social Concerns

—Is student-to-student coitus encouraged through the mandatory use of coed bedrooms and showers?

—Are despondent underachievers and social rejects still throwing themselves off the bell tower?

—That group of students who just went by dressed like nuns—is that a religious thing or an example of a strong conforming culture on campus?

—What sort of social statement do those flaming mattresses represent?

—If everyone's supposed to be so smart at this college, why is everyone wearing flip-flops during a snow storm?

—What's the story with all the Asians?

## Academic Concerns

—If the stuff discussed in that class I visited was too hard for me, won't it almost certainly be way too hard for my child? In fact, I couldn't tell what the subject was, or even what department we were in.

—The Christmas break begins November 11 and ends February 6. What in God's name are we supposed to do with our already too-large-for-the-house child during that period?

—Are Paradise Island or Las Vegas really proper places for a semester abroad? Is Las Vegas even abroad?

—That depraved course, "The Shock of Naked Nudism," that I heard about on Fox News—which building is that in?

—Is it true that part of the fraternity hazing ritual here is to make pledges teach survey courses to freshmen?

## Questions to Ask Yourself

—Considering what other parents look like, do I seem to be dressed and coiffed appropriately?

—Why is the student tour guide such a jerk? Do they manufacture nerds like him here? Why does he keep trying to prove to us why he's qualified to attend a top-flight school?

—Will my child feel lost without a paint-gun battleground nearby?

—Is there always such a bad traffic bottleneck at the highway exit leading into town?

—Why is college so fucking expensive?

# The College Interview

## Yes, Your Child Can Blow the Interview

One of the most important things for you to realize is that you can do everything in your power to help your child with academics and extracurriculars, with résumé building, with standardized tests and the application process—*and he or she can still flush all your good work down the toilet in five minutes with a bad interview.*

"We try not to tell kids this, or let their parents know, but at a significant number of schools, the interview (along with SAT scores and, of course, celebrity recommendations) is the single most important indicator in the admissions process," one college official told me. "A bad interview can kill you. In fact, it's possible to blow the interview to the extent that we will call other top colleges and recommend they also reject the applicant."

I have also discovered that while many good schools say an interview is not a mandatory part of the application process, it really is. And even if they say they no longer conduct interviews, they really do. They secretly expect your child to show up and nail it, preferably by showing them something they've never seen before. What follows is advice on how to do just that.

## Your Child's Appearance

You can't control what happens during the interview, but you can at least try to control how your child looks going in. Most college-admissions books and consultants will tell you that fancy duds are no longer expected for these sessions—which is precisely why I recommend them. You want your child to make an impression. You want to inject a note of seriousness and respect. Why not rent a tux? Why not have your daughter wear the dress she wore to grandma's funeral? What would happen if your son were to glide into his interview in black tie, pull a silver cigarette case out of an inside breast pocket, and offer the dean a smoke? Can you say *Hello, freshman class?*

Of course, most kids don't possess the moxie to pull off such a stunt. For them, I'd suggest a distinctive fashion accessory that will still serve to separate them from the herd:

**The one-hit-wonder rock band T-shirt.** Try to find something that will appeal to an older campus sensibility and perhaps even start a discussion. Zager and Evans, Hurricane Smith, Steam, Lemon Pipers, Oingo Boingo, etc.

**Something for the head.** I earlier mentioned one dean who professed admiration for any applicant who'd have the nerve to wear a sombrero to an interview, but there are many other options that could potentially pack a similar wallop. A fez adds an undeniable air of intrigue, for example, as does a turban, a somber black veil, or a burka. Some admissions officials will look positively on a nurse's or stewardess's cap, while others favor a construction worker's or fireman's hard hat. On the other hand, a propeller beanie or an enormous foam cowboy hat might be seen as needlessly frivolous.

Keep in mind: an accessory is fine, a costume is going too far. An eye patch works well, but not a parrot on the shoulder. A hearing aid is a nice touch, but insisting on speaking in sign language when you don't even know it yourself is excessive.

## Ten General Don'ts

Drill your child with these special no-no's as you both make your way up the sidewalk to the admissions office:

—Don't try to crush the interviewer's hand with your handshake.

—Look the interviewer in the eye, but don't get into a staring contest.

—Don't excuse yourself for a bowel movement in the middle of the interview, no matter how badly you have to go.

—Don't make ridiculous, gratuitous comments, like "Gee, I didn't know you were married to Miss Universe!" while pointing to a photograph of the admissions officer's wife.

—Don't cross your legs at the knees and then again at the ankles.

—Don't begin every answer with a private little chuckle.

—Don't get up and sit on the interviewer's desk or jab at her chest in order to drive home a point.

—Don't make statements that could be deemed life threatening.

—Don't answer every question with a question, i.e. Interviewer: "What do you want to tell me about yourself?" Applicant: "What do you want to tell me about *yourself?*" Interviewer: "Why should we accept you?" Applicant: "Why *shouldn't* you accept me?"

—Don't under any circumstances display your underarms.

## Get Your Child's Grammar Straight/Try Out Some New Words

Wouldn't it be a waste not to use this important interview as an occasion for your child to show off all she learned in high school and in preparation for the SAT and other standardized tests? In stating her case for admission, she shouldn't be afraid to use the full array of prepositions, transitive and intransitive verbs, clauses and phrases of every stripe, helping verbs, conjunctions, interjections, and both direct and indirect objects. Several admissions officers with whom I spoke admitted a special fondness for gerunds. "Whenever I hear one, I look for the accompanying glint in the eye that lets me know it wasn't an accident," said one. "There are few greater thrills."

At the same time, the applicant should be on the sharp lookout for an interviewer who will try to trick her with questions designed to make her stumble grammatically. For instance, if the interviewer asks, "How do you like high school?" he or she is no doubt just trying to trick your child into saying, "I enjoy it very good." Be sure to have her respond instead with the more lyrical, "High school? Enjoy it I do." A little further along in the interview, the interviewer may try another ambush with "What did you do last summer?" The answer shouldn't be, "Me went to the beach." Have her go with something that lends a little mystery, like, "The beach and I got together."

Similarly, this is the perfect opportunity for your child to try out for the first time some of the new words she learned for the SAT verbal section. If she can sprinkle "adumbrate," "puissant," and "gainsay" into a discussion about what her high-school class is doing to save the rain forest, you've got a candidate for early admission!

## College Admissions Officers Talk About the Interview

"If I sneeze, I really expect the applicant to say, 'God bless you.'"

"I don't think it's fair to interview an applicant who has no chance of getting into the school. I tell them as soon as they come in, 'You've got no shot here.' I think they appreciate it in the long run and it certainly makes my day easier."

"Sometimes, if we've got a real backup of applicants waiting to be interviewed, I'll finish a kid's sentences for him."

"I'll admit it. I'm a sucker for a great tattoo, especially on the forehead."

"I don't like it when they just curl up into a ball and start whimpering. The first few times, it was different enough to be effective, and I recommended admission. But now everyone seems to be doing it. It's just not a substitute for talking."

"If the applicant has cough drops, how about offering one to me?"

"There's no question in my mind but that an experienced interviewer can conduct a good interview and check and answer e-mail at the same time. This shouldn't even be a concern."

"It's amazing how many kids want to talk about sports. I hate sports. And extracurricular activities. I hate that stuff, too."

"I always like to begin each day of interviewing with a secret 'magic word.' If the applicant says it—it could be an unlikely one like 'oracle' or 'persimmon,' or a more common word like 'car'—they get a thumb's-up recommendation from me."

# The Mock Interview

Your child can engage in mock interviews with peers who are also applying to college, but these sessions tend to disintegrate with alarming speed, as questions such as "Who are you seeing now?" and "Why are your parents so intense?" take the place of more useful material. In addition, a group of peers may say they want to help your child prepare for his interview, but they're really more interested in creating an embarrassing video that they can send out on youtube.com.

It's far more effective in the long run for you to interview your child yourself. Who better to probe knowledgably into his psyche and bring out the best in him? Who better to keep him alert and "on task" for an entire half hour?

Whatever you do, however, don't take a casual approach. It may be called a "mock" interview, but you should make it as close to the real deal as you can. Select an underused room in your house and furnish it with books, diplomas, and an autographed oar to make it look like a dean's office. Better yet, book a guest room at a local hotel or motel and then have your child "appear" at the door at an agreed-upon time. It is very important for you at this point to pretend you have never met him or her before. Shake hands, chat briefly about the weather or last night's ballgame, discuss friends you may have in common, and then move to your positions across the "desk" from each other.

A typical first exchange might go something like this:

Q: Tell me about your current high school.

A: We're the Wildcats. Purple and white.

Q: I meant more like what are your academic interests? Do you have an idea about what you might major in?

A: Major?

Q: I mean what subjects do you like?

A: I'm pretty cool with them all. History could be better, though. The teacher wears his tie way too tight.

Q: Oh? That's interesting. What does it mean?

A: It makes his neck like . . . bulge out.

Q: Does that make him a bad teacher?

A: Well, it looks like his head is gonna explode. It's hard to take him serious.

Q: Seriously.

A: You could like ask anyone.

Q: No, I meant you should say "seriously" instead of "serious."

A: Whatever.

Before long, the need for these mock interviews becomes obvious. It may seem expensive, but returning to the motel room on four or five occasions should result in an improvement each time (and who's to say one of you can't go ahead and stay the night?).

Considering the importance of this step in the application process, as I've revealed earlier, it's a cost well worth incurring.

---

### The Tip

The question of how much to tip an interviewer, or whether it's appropriate to tip at all, has come up with more urgency as the admissions game has intensified in recent years—and I am prepared to report a finding that's exclusive to the pages of *How to Get a Monkey into Harvard*. My research among school officials and parents tells me that tipping has indeed become de rigueur at top colleges, a bit less so among the lower tiers. No one claims to love this new development, but admissions personnel confide it's yet another way that distinctions can be made in an increasingly competitive field, while parents chalk it up as just another necessary expense in an already costly proposition, like adding a moon roof to the cost of a new car. One couple from Long Island noticed that the process became far simpler for them when they began to think of the interviewing process as a big, big meal at a fancy restaurant, with the interviewer as their child's waiter, the dean of admissions as the captain or maitre d', and the office receptionist as the wine steward. "We spread it around pretty good," reported the father. "No one turned it down." The going rate: 10 percent of one semester's tuition for the interviewer, 3 percent for the dean and 1 or 2 percent for the receptionist.

What application folder wouldn't be enhanced by a half recommendation / half mash note from Heidi Klum or a vaguely threatening postcard from O.J. Simpson?

# 6

# The Application and Recommendations

## The Application

Here at last is the one facet of your child's college-admission process that you can control entirely. It consists of a form that you can fill out and questions you can answer, as well as an essay that you can write. In fact, if you don't mind forging your child's signature at the bottom, there's really no need to get him or her involved at all.

There are two kinds of applications. First, there's the application specifically designed at great effort and expense by and for the college your child is applying to. Second, there's the so-called Common Application, a generic document that in the minds of many reflects the "dumbing down" and homogenization of our culture. Most top colleges say they are perfectly happy to accept the Common Application, but they're really not. They hate it and everything it stands for. How would you like it if there were only one common newspaper for the entire country, or one style of shoe that everyone had to wear, or only one kind of candy in the vending machine? Well, that's the way the

73

colleges feel about what they spitefully refer to as the "Application—not." In short, they give far more credit to applicants who use the school's own application. "If I'm having a particularly bad morning," said one West Coast dean, "I'll just toss all the Common Applications straight into the rejection pile. And I seriously doubt I'm the only one who does this." Her colleague then chimed in, "The applications are common and so are the people who fill them out."

Getting to the body of the application, there are college guides that actually offer assistance on how to fill out your child's name, address, name of high school, courses taken, activities, and so on. "Use a pen," they say. "Spell words correctly." To which I can only add, "Duh" and "Duh."

Of some seeming interest are the short-answer questions ("What's your favorite planet? Why?" or "Describe your favorite recurring dream"), but the colleges openly admit these are mere space eaters, not seriously read by anyone. As such, you might let your child take a crack at one or two of these in the unlikely event that he's starting to feel shut out from the process.

## Supplementary Materials

Sometimes the completed application form just doesn't seem to do justice to all the applicant has to offer. In this case, admissions officials are happy to consider supplemental materials you truly believe will help your child's chances of admission. The most common among these add-ons are lottery scratch-off tickets, usually five or ten of them, and possibly a few Powerball tickets if the jackpot is especially high. These are of course always welcome but you must accept the fact that the chances of a large payoff (either for the admissions official or your child) are slim. Will a two- or three-dollar prize be enough to get your child into a top school? Well, all other things being equal . . .

Other extras I've heard can tip the balance in a close decision are gift certificates (ten dollars or more) to McDonald's or Dunkin' Donuts, tire-pressure gauges that fit on a key ring, little bundles of resin-soaked kindling, scented candles, rubberized jar openers, and elongated lighters for fireplaces and outdoor grills.

# The Essay

Thomas Carlyle wrote essays. Charles Lamb (under the pen name Elia) wrote essays. Susan Sontag wrote essays. Basically, a lot of people, now dead, wrote essays back in what our young people would call "the day." So why on earth, you may well ask, would top colleges—whose business it is to keep both eyes squarely on the future—continue to indulge in such a creaky exercise, especially when they know the applicants themselves rarely do any of the actual writing?

"We ask ourselves that question every year," I was told by the dean of admissions at a top school in upstate New York. "Are they doing essays in China? We know they're not. Japan? No way. In any of the other countries that are kicking our asses economically? No. So why is it still the nineteenth century in America? Should we also have a box on the application asking students if they've been inoculated against smallpox?"

And yet the essay persists and remains a steady, troubling background noise in the application process. As we have already established, the SAT score is the only thing we know that *all* colleges look at (along with any celebrity recommendations you can produce, *see below*), but a very good or very bad essay sometimes pops into view almost inadvertently. My advice is that it's probably worth doing one and doing it well. You can either have your child write an essay that you will completely rewrite, or you can just write the whole thing from scratch yourself.

## Essay Topics

Most applications will ask candidates for admission to submit an essay of two hundred and fifty to three hundred words on one of several suggested topics. You may get the impression that because there are several topics, you have a choice of which one to address. In truth, however, the college would greatly prefer that you answer the first question on the list. It's a classic question, always, and one that doesn't change much from year to year. Here's how it appeared on one Ivy League college's application in 2006:

> *Using specific words and phrases from your own experience, what has been the significance of the importance in ways that give meaning to this special influence?*

As you can see, this topic is designed to draw all sorts of different responses. According to an admissions officer at the school in question, some students used it to discuss their own attempted suicides or battles with eating disorders. Others talked about cutting themselves, and total strangers, with razor blades, vandalizing public property, or coming on sexually to teachers and high school custodial workers. All of which demonstrates yet again why it is imperative that you control your own child's application process—and work on the essay yourself.

## Essay Tips

You've got the topic for the essay, but that doesn't mean you just begin writing off the top of your head. Or does it? Stream of consciousness writing, or automatic writing, may be somewhat out of favor right now in the literary world, but that may be all the more reason to give it a try. I'd suggest that an admissions committee (made up mostly of humanities majors, remember) will deal quite favorably with an essay that begins:

> Able I was ere I saw Elbow—little man at ElbaBeachClub whining while dining as I wandered down the splashy strand crazy as a loon in the happledapple light of a cockeyed moonfaced dune. Growing they growl grow! but it's gnawing at me knowing the ivory tower's crowing and me here all alone entreating in *letmeinmotif*: let me in . . .

Not quite your child's voice? There are several other literary styles that will just as likely catch the committee's eye. Heroic couplets, for example, are almost never used, nor are French alexandrines or the simple, urgent declarative sentences of airliner black-box recorders.

As you proceed with you child's essay, there are several other thing to keep in mind as you go:

**Watch out for anachronisms.** Remember the case of Mrs. Anna Stimson of suburban Chicago, who made the news after she screwed up her child's application to Tufts by putting in references to swine flu shots! You really can't write knowledgably or nostalgically about TV programs like "The Carol Burnett Show" or dances like the Bump without tipping your hand.

**Be honest but not too honest.** Did your child help raise money for guide dogs? Yes indeed. But how did that five hundred dollars turn into fifty thousand? Ooops! Typing error! My bad!

**Reuse a sibling's essay.** Did an older brother or sister get into a top college? If so, a little recycling may be in order. Just be sure to change gender references where appropriate.

**Avoid politically incorrect words and phrases.** Admissions committees these days are very, very sensitive (some would even say hypersensitive) on this subject, so avoid phrases like "as drunk as an Irishman," "as tight as a tick," and even "as happy as a lark." Similarly, try to stay away from "Scotch tape," "Dutch oven," "French kiss," and "American flag."

## Essay: The Last Line

There's certainly no shortage of help being offered these days to young people and their parents, faced with a college-application essay. The advice comes in many forms, too. Some "experts" specialize in suggesting topics for the essay, others offer to edit it. Some online services even offer to write the whole thing for a fee. But no one, with all their fancy advice, ever seems to touch on what I believe is the essay's most important element of all: the closing line.

The conclusion of the essay is what the readers take with them into the admissions-committee meetings. It's the last thing they remember about you and your best chance to make a lasting impression. Therefore, I am pleased to offer you and your child a number of what I consider to be sure-fire last lines. It will be your task, of course, to compose the words that lead up to these final lines, but I suspect you're up to it. And if not, you can always hire someone. The lines are:

1. "And that's how I learned once and for all that a faggot is really nothing more than a pile of sticks."

2. "One blink means 'yes,' two means 'no' . . . and three means 'I love you.'"

3. "Uma rolled over and went to sleep at last, completely satisfied for the first time in her life."

4. "If you think early admissions are so unfair, why don't you go tell it to Harvard," my advisor said. And so I did.

5. "With a fireman over each shoulder, I at last emerged safely into what had become the moonscape of lower Manhattan."

6. "And that," he told me in conclusion, "is how I came to write *Gravity's Rainbow*."

7. "A library? With my name on it? But where should I put it, Daddy?"

## Recommendations

Traditionally, the applicant goes to several of his or her teachers or other figures of authority and asks them to write a recommendation. This, I have to tell you, is a nearly worthless exercise in the eyes of most admissions officials. The typical teacher has to write dozens of recommendations every year. How much effort do you suppose they put into them? How much do you think they bother to differentiate between your A student and the freak who sat atop the school flagpole for ten days last spring? Well, guess what? It's even worse than you think.

"I'm certain that most parents would be shocked if they saw what teachers really write on these things," one dean told me.

"They mock the students, they doodle, they write down groceries they need, or calculate monthly loan payments. Very frequently, they get the recommendations mixed up or forget to send them at all."

So as you prepare your child's application, maybe it's time to rethink recommendations entirely. Forget the teachers, coaches, and school administrators. Forget the alums who never really liked the school to begin with. Here are a couple of fresh approaches to recommendations that just might get the admissions committee on your child's side.

## The Celebrity Recommendation

It's tremendously important to keep in mind that admissions officials are human beings with the same interests and desires the rest of us have. Consequently, they are as starstruck by big names and famous faces as anyone. If you can secure a recommendation from a celebrity, even something scrawled on a publicity glossy or a cocktail napkin, your child will have an instant advantage over all the applicants who are submitting droning letters from their calculus teachers.

Which celebrities to choose? The whole idea here is glamour and glitz. Don't bother with a fusty old Nobel laureate in Literature or the host of a PBS science or cooking program, no matter how accessible they may seem. What you want are Hollywood babes and hunks, aging rock stars, athletes, and supermodels of the universe. What application folder wouldn't be enhanced by a half recommendation/half mash note from Heidi Klum or a vaguely threatening postcard from O. J. Simpson?

Of course, these favors come with a price tag attached. You won't get away for less then five hundred dollars with O.J., for example, while a seemingly thoughtful note from Meryl Streep might go as high as three thousand. On the other hand, former president Jimmy Carter has long had a set price of a hundred dollars, with lower charges in cases of demonstrated need. Here is a short list of 2007 prices just to give you an idea of the range:

| Ludacris          | $1,500              |
| Ed McMahon        | $30                 |
| Frank Rich        | $300                |
| Pete Rose         | $10 (plus postage)  |
| Margaret Thatcher | $5,000              |
| Pat Benatar       | $600                |

## The Parental Recommendation

"Well, why not?" you wonder to yourself. Admissions officers act as if the last people on earth they want to hear from are the applicant's parents—but who better to summarize all the child's attributes, clearly state the contributions he'd make to the life of the college in question, and explain away his failures and faults as charming idiosyncrasies? Why should the parent of all people be left out at this crucial juncture—at what will surely be the child's one last time of need?

My feeling here is a sympathetic one. Too much is left to chance when others (virtual strangers, in some cases) supply these recommendations to admissions committees. When all is said and done, the only way to make sure they get the real story is to write it yourself. By the way, this is likely to become more of a trend in the years to come, as parents run out of new gimmicks to try. So if you're going to do it, do it now.

---

### The Many Faces of Rejection

As an attentive, ambitious parent, you are no doubt familiar with the various gimmicks—Early Action, Early Decision, Rolling Admission, and so on—that admissions officers have cooked up to help keep themselves interested in what can become a pretty tedious process. But one shocking development you don't know about—and which I am pleased to claim as yet another *Monkey* exclusive—comes from a piece of paper I innocently fished out of an admissions-department wastebasket in a large Rhode Island city. The document, a photocopy of an original that had been initialed by the deans at fourteen prominent

Charles Monagan 81

Northeastern colleges, was nothing less than a secret strategy for the *rejection* of top-college applicants. It seems that these schools now spend so much time and effort rejecting applicants ("I really should be called the Dean of Rejection," admitted one college official) that they felt the need for new guidelines and essentially a new "language of rejection." In the document, the deans agreed to hew to certain new standards as they hack through the ranks of unqualified, unfit, or otherwise delusional high-school seniors. Here are a few of the newly agreed-upon terms as laid out in the document I found:

**Early Discouragement.** This is to be the first bump in the road for an unqualified applicant. E-mails to the admissions office are not returned, phone calls are put on interminable hold, and the applicant's name is intentionally misspelled in what little correspondence there is. In test cases, many of those receiving this treatment were put off enough so they never followed through with a full application.

**Instant Rejection.** This rejection by return mail sends a very strong signal to the applicant, namely: *What were you thinking? We are not even going to go through the charade of waiting until our "early" acceptance/rejection date!* Instant Rejection is a more popular ploy than Early Discouragement because even though the rejection is forceful and final, the school still receives the full application fee.

**"Red Card" Rejection.** Going into the annual round of decision making, each admissions official will be given three "red cards" that can be pulled and displayed at any point in the process to veto a candidate. No reason need be given for flashing the card and no questions are allowed from other committee members.

**Social Rejection.** Many students are very highly qualified when it comes to academic performance, but are such total dweebs that even the thought of them skulking around in the shadows on a glorious fall afternoon or studying in their rooms on a big party weekend is more than most admissions committees can bear. *Take your box of Triscuits and go study at some other school!*

**Blanket Rejection.** Reserved for applicants so weak or obnoxious or otherwise unlikable that their names go straight into the fourteen-school computer database, rejected by one and all with no hope of reconsideration.

# Afterword

And so there you have it—the sum of my efforts on behalf of you and your child as you proceed down the road to college admission. Some of you have quite rightly asked over the years about my own children, and my own efforts and results in getting *them* into top schools. Well, the truth is that I never had much luck with the ladies. I never found one to call my own, and now it's getting late enough in the game to think I never will. No marriage, no children, no framed photos on the piano, no personal college-admission stories to tell in my dotage.

But this means I've been able to devote all my time to you and your child and to "adopt" many of you as my own. I look forward to hearing your stories and putting some of them into my next book, a novel about animal-rights activists.

Until then, I wish you the best of luck in your efforts. Please remember to give your dopey child a slap on the back of the head for me!

# A Two-Year College-Admissions Timeline

## Junior Year

### September

Review your child's curriculum. Remember what we've stressed: easy classes rule! Now is the time to request a transfer from that nasty AP Biology into the far simpler ADD History: Honoring Old Glory.

This is also the time to review your child's extracurriculars. As we have learned, it's not a question of what she's good at, it's what she *looks* good at.

Continue reviewing for next month's PSATs. In your vocabulary study, remember to have your child "live the word" for a day. Is the word "gesticulation"? He needs to spend the day pointing and signaling.

### October

The PSATs. What are these tests exactly? No one pays any attention to the results except for the wise owls at the Illinois-based

National Merit Scholarship Corporation, who claim to hand out money to those who do well. *But do they really??*

College fair season. Beware of mascots bearing candy.

Have your child join his classmates and watch them as they plant bulbs in the planters on Main Street for the extracurricular beautification project. He can get full credit without doing any of the actual work!

The blizzard of unsolicited e-mails and brochures continues to arrive from fallback colleges that have your child listed because he took last year's PSATs.

## November

While driving around town, begin the mental process of "seeing" what it would be like for your child (and, by extension, you) to attend various schools. Project forward to the conversations you'll have:

"So where is Freddy this fall?"

"Cornell."

How does that word "Cornell" sound to you? How does it fall from your lips? Do you feel natural and comfortable with it? What is the other person's reaction to it? Do you detect any envy there? Assess. Repeat with the name of another school.

## December

The opportunities for enrichment courses are running out as your child moves quickly through high school. The holiday break is an excellent time to enroll him or her in an "Introductory Magic" course at your local community college or Holiday Inn. The basics are not hard to learn, and I have never known an admissions officer *not* to be impressed with a sleight of hand or really good card trick during an interview. I heard of one case in which a fun-loving dean actually let himself be sawed in half. Needless to say, the applicant was accepted on the spot.

PSAT scores come back. You really didn't expect your child to be a Merit Scholarship Finalist, did you? Don't lower your college sights, though. Not yet. It might just have been a bad day.

## January

Here comes the first round of SATs. No turning back now. It's kind of like your wedding day: all that planning and preparation only to have it come and go in a flash. It's an unusual request, but see if you can get permission to shoot a video of your child as she breaks the seal on the examination booklet. Embarrassment? Who cares? You worked very hard for this moment! In fact, why don't you have the monitor take a shot of you and your child together as she fills in the first answer?

Time to make those summer plans. Will it be another "internship" at Burger King? Might as well be, because admissions committees pay no attention at all to summer activities. You have to remember that they went to work at a school primarily for one reason: to have their summers off. As far as they're concerned, if you're not off on vacation somewhere watching the clouds roll by, you're a sucker.

Plan your child's senior-year courses. Remember: An easy A is the way!

## February

Make your first college visits. Don't look at it as a chance to get to know your child, or you will be disappointed. Nor is it the time to haul out your old college story of jumping out a second-floor window, running to a neighboring dorm, and hiding in a closet for three hours to avoid getting nabbed in a glue-sniffing bust.

If your child took the SAT I in January, the results come in now. Maybe it's time to lower your sights just a little, but still no reason to panic.

Take a first look at the FAFSA, the federal government's financial information form, on the Web Worksheet just to familiarize yourself with how ridiculous and tedious it is.

## March

Time to redouble or even retriple or requadruple your child's preparations for the spring SAT I and SAT II. Not to mention the stupid AP tests, if you have somehow gotten involved with them (there was no need!). Everyone knows someone who knows someone who works miracles with difficult SAT cases, but upon further investigation the thirty-five-thousand-dollar fee seems a little steep. Much better just to get those big, colorful, dog-eared SAT review books out of the drawer once more.

Spring Break. Your child will want to prepare for college by going off to some godforsaken place on the Gulf Coast where they guzzle fruity vodka drinks through a garden hose and then get all sweaty and start kissing members of their own sex. You will have to think of at least one good reason why she shouldn't.

Athletes should begin contacting college coaches. *Athletes.* If your child is batting .185 or is the high school's number-two JV high jumper or keeps hitting her backhand into the neighboring court, coaches at the next level don't need to hear about it.

## April

Time to start identifying the people you and your child will ask for letters of recommendation. As we have learned, admissions officials generally do not read teacher recommendations, while letters from alumni can often have a negative impact on an application. Aside from celebrity recommendations, which always work, you might go for an offbeat approach. A simple note from a crossing guard or children's department shoe salesman who remembers your child from years ago might have some contrarian appeal.

Discuss college costs with your child. Explain that you are planning to spend roughly two hundred thousand dollars and that at some point in the future you'd like to be repaid.

## May

Time for the SATs once again. Some advisors don't think much of hypnotism as a way to prepare, but I see nothing wrong with it. We mustn't forget the uproar that occurred several years ago in suburban Baltimore when a test taker got his hypnotist's signals crossed and started clucking like a chicken and pretending to lay eggs on a neighboring desk.

Go to the whip hand for these final weeks of the school year. Begin daily contact with all your child's teachers, advisors, and school administrators in an effort to bring all grades up a notch or two. Of course, they're all familiar with you after literally years of close contact and at this point can basically smell you coming.

## Senior Year

### September

Don't forget that the new Early, Early Action and Early, Early Decision deadlines come up on or around Labor Day. These handy applications come with "Accept" and "Reject" stickers that school officials simply affix and send back. A rejection allows your child to still seek Early Decision or Not-Quite-So-Early Decision elsewhere.

Chart your standardized test course for October and November. Your child will take the SAT I again, of course, and one or more SAT II Subject Tests, and you could throw in a couple of ACTs as well. Or you might line up an "ACT sandwich," in which she takes the ACT, then an SAT II, then an SAT I, and finishes things off with another ACT. An "SAT II sandwich" would of course envelop an ACT and a savory SAT I within the warm folds of a couple of SAT IIs. There is no "SAT sandwich," but an "SAT hero" is someone (usually an athlete trying to make a qualifying score for college) who takes every available SAT during his junior and senior years.

### October

Check the entertainment pages of your local paper to see what movies will be coming out this fall and holiday season so you can determine which film actors to contact for celebrity recommendations for your child. Admissions officials are susceptible to any contact from stars who are currently "hot."

Pick that perfect fall day to visit the college you most want your child to attend. Even an inattentive male will somehow sense (but not quite communicate) that it's a nice place worth considering.

Remind your child to begin dropping out of the school organizations she'd joined strictly for the sake of building up her résumé.

## November

Here we go with the freakin' SATs again. Where does all the money go that you and millions of others pay for the tests and the extra few bucks that many parents now pay so their children can get the scores back a little early? Well, some of those estates in Princeton are pretty fancy.

Begin practicing your child's signature so you'll be able to sign his or her application with authority.

## December

All applications should be completed and sent out before the holiday break. Avoid the frivolous application by remembering that Yale last year made over a million dollars on application fees from prospects who were rejected.

Popular holiday gifts for admissions officers include expensive mail-order fruit boxes and steaks, CD or DVD boxed sets, vouchers for flying anywhere within the continental U.S., or those furry steering-wheel covers.

## January

There's nothing more that you can do. Other guides will give you the impression that there's still work to be done during the senior winter and spring, but it's all window dressing. Take your foot off the gas. And take the other one out of your child's rear end.